What they d

TUD~~OR~~S

By Bob Fowke

Dedicated to Henry VIII,
who kept his head when
all about him were losing theirs.

*Hodder
Children's
Books*

A division of Hodder Headline Limited

Hello.
My name's Will
Somers. I was
Henry VIII's jester. I
had to cheer him up
when he felt gloomy.

He used to tell me things
no-one else knew.

Read on if you want to find
out the true facts about
old King Henry and his
Tudor chums.

This edition of *What They Don't Tell You About Henry VIII* and *What They Don't Tell You About Elizabeth I* first published by Hodder Children's Books 2001.

Cover: Portrait of Henry VIII (1491–1547) c. 1525–30 (panel) by English School (16th century). Philip Mould, Historical Portraits Ltd, London, UK/Bridgeman Art Library.

What They Don't Tell You About Henry VIII first published as a single volume in Great Britain in 1995 by Hodder Children's Books.

Copyright © 1995 Lazy Summer Books

The right of Lazy Summer Books to be identified as the authors of the Work has been asserted by them in accordance with the Copyright, Designs and Patents Act 1988.

10 9 8 7 6 5 4 3 2 1

ISBN 0 340 78808 9

A Catalogue record for this book is available from the British Library.

Printed by The Guernsey Press Ltd, Guernsey, Channel Islands.

Hodder Children's Books
A division of Hodder Headline Limited
338 Euston Road
London NWI 3BH

CONTENTS

 Whenever you see this sign in the book it means there are some more details at the FOOT of the page, like here.

3

HOORAY HENRY!

STEP ASIDE FOR A REAL KING

England, 1509. A peaceful land of green fields, and pretty milkmaids milking dozy cows. A land of peace. All is calm, as people carry out their work for the lord of the manor, the bishops and the Pope.

In London a great celebration is taking place, because England has a handsome new King. Everyone is happy because a bright new age is dawning.

Or is it?....

SPOT THE DIFFERENCE
BEFORE

At the start, Henry had it all. Power. Looks. Strength. Intelligence. Wealth. Popularity. He was religious, artistic and sporty. He had lots of energy and loved parties.

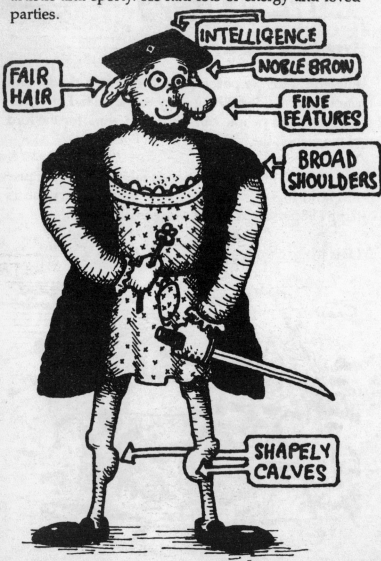

INTELLIGENCE

NOBLE BROW

FAIR HAIR

FINE FEATURES

BROAD SHOULDERS

SHAPELY CALVES

AFTER

Nearly forty years later, Henry had become a bad-tempered old man. He was so fat he had to be lowered onto his horse with a rope and a pulley.

EYES CLOSING OVER

HEADACHES

PUFFY FACE

1·4 METRE WAIST

ULCERS

So What Went Wrong?

Henry got fat because he never stopped eating huge meals, most of them meat dishes. He thought that eating huge amounts showed how important he was.

His headaches may have been the result of jousting in his youth. In the end, his favourite sport became so dangerous that he had to give it up, and he became more and more of a throne potato.

It wasn't just his looks that went to pot; his personality changed as well. He started off as a pleasant man, and finished up as a monster who couldn't stand anyone disagreeing with him.

How on earth did such a man get to the throne of England in the first place?

TUDOR TROUBLE

It all began about a hundred years earlier, when a Welshman called Owen Tudor signed up to fight with King Henry V. Owen took part in a great English victory over the French at Agincourt.

After the battle, Henry V married the French princess Catherine of Valois, 'Sweet Kate'. But Henry V died when Catherine was only twenty-one, leaving her at a loose end. Her son, a nine-month old boy called Henry VI, became King of England. Powerful uncles stepped in to look after the country.

One day, Kate heard that the Welsh captain, Owen Tudor, was having secret meetings with one of her ladies-in-waiting. Royals don't like courtiers to have secret affairs, so she decided to teach Owen Tudor a lesson and went to meet him instead of her lady-in-waiting. Her trick went wrong because she and Owen fell in love and got married.

You didn't marry the Queen Mum without permission. Owen was put in prison and Kate was sent to a convent where she died young. Later, Owen was allowed to become a royal park keeper in North Wales. He wasn't important enough to behead. Somehow they had four children - children with royal blood in their veins, which is why about fifty years later, after much plotting and fighting, Owen's grandson was able to claim the throne as Henry VII.

Henry VII came to power at the end of the Wars of the Roses. Here are your Roses questions answered.

THE WARS OF THE ROSES

WHAT WERE THE WARS OF THE ROSES?
A long struggle between two families – York and Lancaster for the throne of England. They lasted thirty years.

WHAT WERE THE ROSES?
The house of Lancaster had a red rose as an emblem, and the Yorkists a white one.

WHAT WERE THE DIFFERENCES BETWEEN THE TWO SIDES?
Not much. The Lancastrians were there first and ruled for most of the time, but Yorkist Edward IV was a good soldier and grabbed the throne.

WHO WON?
Henry VII, was a minor Lancastrian. But once he was king, he married Elizabeth of York, so you could say both sides won. He invented the Tudor rose, which was the red Lancastrian and the white Yorkist roses joined together.

TUDOR TIMES

Royal uncles in baby fight   1422

Henry VI, the nine-month-old baby son of Henry V, has been crowned King of England. Several uncles are fighting for power.

King cops it   1471

Henry VI has been murdered after his defeat by the Yorkists, perhaps by his hunchback brother.

Tower princes presumed dead   1483

Following the death of Edward IV, his nasty brother has claimed the throne as Richard III. Two little princes, Edward's sons, have been murdered in the Tower of London.

Welshman gets leg up   1429

Catherine of Valois, the Queen Mum, has married obscure Welsh captain Owen Tudor,   after bedroom tryst trick turned to true love.

Tudor triumphs at Bosworth 1485

Henry Tudor has invaded England for the Lancastrians and killed Richard at the battle of Bosworth Field. He has been crowned Henry VII and has married Elizabeth of York, thus bringing the Wars of the Roses to an end.

Henry bowled by yorker   1461

The Duke of York's son, supported by Warwick the Kingmaker, has grabbed the throne for the house of York. He plans to rule as Edward IV, after smashing the Lancastrian army. Henry VI is still alive so now there are two kings, but only one working.

Simnel sinks to kitchen 1487

Royal pretender, Lambert Simnel has been defeated by Henry VII's forces. Lambert was trying to claim the throne of England for the Yorkists. It is said that his life has been spared and he will be allowed to work in the King's kitchens.

11

AFTER THE PRUNING OF THE ROSES

When Henry VII came to the throne, English people were tired of the endless killing of the Wars of the Roses. What they wanted was peace, and Henry VII gave it to them. Under Henry, the power of the great lords was cut back. The lords were no longer allowed to keep great armies. Henry ruled through Justices of the Peace and tax collectors.

Henry VII was now ruler of a country of less than three million people and most of them lived in the countryside. London was the capital with its splendid Tower of London and Tower Bridge. London was full of rich merchants and young apprentices. Foreigners noticed two things about London – Londoners hated them and the streets were very muddy. Compared, say, to Italy, Henry VII's England was a bit behind the times, but at last it had a tough King.

MEET THE FAMILY

Five tough Tudors wore the crown, beginning with grandad Henry VII and then, toughest of all, his son Henry VIII. Then came three of Henry VIII's children, each from a different wife.

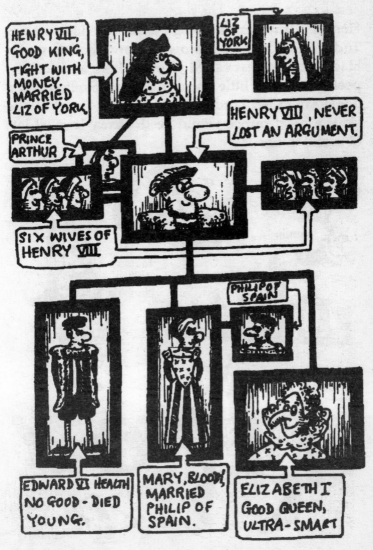

HENRY VII, GOOD KING, TIGHT WITH MONEY. MARRIED LIZ OF YORK.

LIZ OF YORK

HENRY VIII, NEVER LOST AN ARGUMENT.

PRINCE ARTHUR

SIX WIVES OF HENRY VIII

PHILIP OF SPAIN

EDWARD VI HEALTH NO GOOD - DIED YOUNG.

MARY, BLOODY, MARRIED PHILIP OF SPAIN.

ELIZABETH I GOOD QUEEN, ULTRA-SMART

ROYAL TUDOR KIDS

During his father's reign, the future Henry VIII and his elder brother Arthur were growing up. Let's see first what it was like to be a royal kid, and then see how everyone else spent their youth.

Henry VIII never had to go to school. Like all top Tudor kids, he had his own tutor. Henry's was a black-robed priest called John Skelton, an excellent poet who made little use of the birch. Skelton and a nobleman called Lord Mountjoy taught Henry all the skills a royal prince would need. Henry learned lots of useful things.

French and Latin

Tennis

Music and dancing

Chess

The Arts of War

Bowls

Cards

and a bit about gambling

Here's how other Tudor kids got educated:

- No school at all for many poor boys.
- Village or 'dame' school run by an old lady, to teach basics.
- No school for girls.
- Grammar school – run by monks for brighter, or better off pupils. Most of them were shut down in the early Tudor period.

Tudor school pupils had a tough time. But a Tudor teacher's life wasn't too bad. One teacher's day went like this: morning – explain the lesson. Midday – sleep while the pupils did their lesson. Afternoon – listen to their answers.

THWACK!

Yes, for those who went to school during Henry VII's reign, things could get pretty rough.

Punishment was a favourite Tudor pastime, and children were beaten often, whatever the offence. One schoolmaster used to beat his boys in the mornings simply to warm himself up.

School lasted all the daylight hours, and most pupils would walk there and back, often in the dark. They had to wear a cap and take a knife for cutting meat.

At school, there were very few books. (Printed books had only just been invented.) They could use a horn book, which was shaped like a hand mirror. On one side, there were key bits to read, like the alphabet, and on the other they could write. Pupils wrote with quill pens. There might be up to sixty pupils in a class. Pupils would have to learn long passages from text-books. The main subjects were English, Arithmetic, Divinity and Latin. Some schools began to teach Greek.

SCHOOL RULES

Here are some typical Tudor rules:

Don't carry sticks, bats or daggers

Don't lose your cap

Don't tease other pupils

No drinking, cards or dice

No oaths or rude words

Dress tidily and cleanly

Have good table manners

Holidays must have been welcome, especially as there were so few of them – sixteen days at Christmas, twelve at Easter. How many days in the summer? None!

JOBS FOR THE BOYS, HOUSEWORK FOR GIRLS

Growing up in Henry VII's England was much simpler than it is today. Most boys followed their father's way of work. Mostly this was something to do with farming or serving the lord of the manor. But there were other trades –

a village of 100 people might have a blacksmith, a miller, a carpenter, a potter, a weaver and vicar. A town of 1,000 people might have a butcher, baker, tailor, tanner, fishmonger and shoemaker as well. County towns of about 5,000 people would have barbers, silversmiths, merchants, glovers, schoolteachers and lawyers.

Young boys at the age of eight would often be sent away from home to learn a trade with another master. It seems English parents found they got more service and respect from other people's children! The boys who were sent away were called apprentices. Many young people, including girls, spent some time away from home as servants – and most servants were young people.

Most girls became housewives. Until the monasteries and nunneries were closed educated boys and girls could become monks or nuns.

EXPANDING ENGLAND

While young Henry and all the other Tudor kids were growing up, Henry VII got on with the job of running the country. And he did it very well. By the end of his reign when young Henry had grown into a young man, England was richer and more powerful than she had been for a hundred years.

COURT REPORT

Name Henry VII   **Reign** 1458 – 1509

State of country	Excellent. Peace and plenty all round. Well done.
Economy	Very well managed. A jolly good account. Well done.
Family matters	Shrewd plans for children. All well married. Good.
Foreign policy	Safe — too careful to waste money on wars.
Marriages	Happy marriage to Elizabeth of York.
Splendour	Not much. His court was pretty boring towards the end. But he did keep exotic animals like lions and leopards. Ok
General	Henry has performed well. FF, Headmaster

20

COURTLY CAPERS

GETTING CROWNED

When he was still a teenager, Henry's elder brother died, so Henry received the biggest present any English youth could hope for – the crown of England. On 23rd June 1509, he got up at 6 am, then bathed and heard mass. He dressed in special clothes. Underneath, he wore a lawn shirt, a crimson shirt and a coat of crimson satin – all these had openings so that he could be anointed with oil in the right places during his coronation ceremony. Over it all he wore a topcoat with fur and a crimson satin mantle plus a little cap of state.

His coronation was ultra-splendid. People wore robes and trappings described as 'more rich' and 'more curious' than anything ever seen before. The coronation banquet was said to be better than any feast of the Roman Emperors.

At Westminster Abbey the attendants were 'asked' if they would accept the King, while the Archbishop of Canterbury made the sign of the cross with oil 'in the palms of his hands, on his breast, between his shoulders, and on the blades of his arms'. Then Henry was given the royal crown, ring, sceptre and orb.

Anointed means having special oil, or some other sacred liquid poured on you ceremonially.

HIS FIRST MARRIAGE

Ten days before he was crowned, Henry married his long term fiancée Catherine of Aragon, the King of Spain's daughter.

Catherine of Aragon had already been married to Henry's older brother, Arthur, who'd died. At least Arthur and Catherine had been through a wedding ceremony, it is true, but there are different stories about whether they actually lived together as man and wife.

After Arthur died, Catherine was engaged to Henry, but as he was only twelve at the time, she was kept more or less locked up until he grew up. Catherine was six years older. Henry married Catherine ten days before his coronation, so they could be crowned together.

PASTIME, PASTIME, PASTIME

Catherine was small and pretty and Henry was in love with her. He said "If I were still free, I would still choose her for wife before all others".

All was sunny at their royal court. Henry was seventeen years old. Everyone was going to have fun, and never mind the expense. His silly old ministers would find the money. To make himself popular, he had his father's taxmen, Empson and Dudley, executed. What fun it all was.

Henry loved music, dance, clothes, hunting, wrestling, pretty women, food, drink, gambling and ideas. All this fun he called 'pastime'. He even wrote songs about it. Life was one long party as Henry and Catherine moved between their palaces of Westminster, Greenwich, Richmond, Windsor and the Tower. Palaces got so dirty they soon needed a thorough cleaning. That's one reason why they kept moving.

HER HOUSEHOLD

Catherine was looked after by a hundred and sixty people, including eight ladies-in-waiting as well as ladies of the bedchamber. She had very few Spaniards with her. Catherine wanted to be as English as possible.

HIS HOUSEHOLD

Meanwhile, Henry's Lord Steward had to prepare banquets for up to 1,000 people at a time. Altogether, Henry was looked after by about five hundred people plus a royal guard of three hundred.

DRESSING UP AND DRESSING DOWN

TOP PEOPLE

Henry was as vain as a peacock and wanted to look better than Francis I, the French king. Everyone at Henry and Catherine's court wore rich clothes. The men strutted their stuff in doublet and hose, with a codpiece ━ and padded pantaloons.

Top Tudor women talked in high childish voices to sound cute. They wore a petticoat and bodice, with a gown over. A new fashion was the French hood. It showed, daringly, a bit of hair. Necklines were low and square. Another new fashion was the farthingale, a kind of hidden frame which filled out the skirt at the sides. Night gowns and night caps were for the evening. Even simpler nightcaps were to sleep in.

A codpiece was a stuffed piece of cloth which stuck out of the front of a man's pantaloons.

Bottom people

Servants and labourers were forbidden to dress smartly. Henry was very fussy about what they wore and passed the Sumptuary Laws, to say what people could wear. The workers had to make do with wool jackets and wool bonnets.

Eat up!

Food was a favourite Tudor pastime for aristocrats. In 1533, Henry visited the Marquess of Exeter in Surrey. The menu included:

FIRST COURSE
Salads such as cabbage, lettuces, purslane, damsons, artichokes and cucumbers and cold meats like duck, stewed sparrows, carp, larded pheasants, gulls, forced rabbit, pasty of venison (fallow deer), pear pasty.

SECOND COURSE (HOT)
Stork, heron, quail, partridge, fresh sturgeon, pasty of venison (red deer), baked chickens, fritters.

THIRD COURSE
Jelly, blancmange, apples with pistachios, pears with caraway, scraped cheese with sugar, quince pie.

AFTERS
Wafers and hippocras (spiced wine)

Cooked vegetables were rare. Meat and fish were often cooked with herbs and spices to hide the fact that they were not fresh, or that they had been preserved with salt. All this food needed huge kitchens, and a huge staff to prepare and serve the food.

HOMES AND HOUSES

THE POOR COUNTRYMAN

While Henry and Catherine partied and moved between their palaces, ordinary people lived in simple, wood framed houses filled with wattle and daub (sticks and plaster). Sometimes there would just be one room. The man of the house might have a section curtained off near the fireplace where he did business. He had a chair – the only chair – and sat at a table, the top of which was called a board . This board would have a smooth side, for posh occasions. Then it would be turned over at meal times and people ate off the rough side. The toilet was just a hole in the ground outside the back door. The floor was hard earth, covered in rushes.

In business today we still talk about the chairperson and the board – the other directors who sit round the board-room table and make decisions.

26

Some lived better than others in Henry's England. Wealthy London merchants would have buildings of several floors. They lived above the shop, and their houses might have several rooms – hall, parlour, buttery (kitchen), and storage. There was plenty of wooden furniture – chairs, benches, cupboards, table and sideboard. They'd also have a lot of different clothes for curtains, wall hangings, bed-clothes, cushions, table-clothes. They also had masses of expensive tableware and personal jewellery. Bedrooms tended to be in the attic right under a thatched roof. Bugs and bits of straw used to fall down on the bed, so the beds were four-poster with a canopy over them.

HOUSE HUNTING

Rich Tudor people
were great ones for
building. For
the first time in
England large
houses were
built in stone
or brick. You
can still see
them dotted
around the country.

Henry liked big ones and could persuade people to give them to him – it didn't do to refuse the king. In this way he collected Hampton Court, York Place and Cardinal College.

He told Archbishop Cranmer that he would rather like Knole, one of the more splendid properties belonging to the Archbishop. Cranmer did not want to part with this lovely building, so he suggested Henry might like nearby Otford, which was larger and could cope with all Henry's servants. Henry said he preferred Knole as it was on healthier, higher ground.

Cranmer repeated that Otford would suit Henry better, so then Henry said he would like both places, Knole for himself and a small group of retainers, and Otford for the mass of his servants! He got both, and gave Cranmer a far less valuable property in exchange. Typical Henry.

WELL PLAYED CHAPS!

A-SPORTING WE WILL GO

Henry's England was anything but merry. Working people often had to work from five in the morning until seven at night. Henry banned all sports except archery, which was really military training. He wanted people to work, work, work. Banned games and sports for ordinary folk included:

tennis,
bowls,
skittles,
dice,
cards,
quoits,
and even football.

Things were pretty grim for ordinary people. If you had no work, you could be hanged for vagrancy – and lots of people were out of work. Of course, the upper classes could play as much as they liked, and of course, ordinary people still tried to find ways of having a good time, law or no law.

JOUSTING

Henry's favourite sports were jousting, hunting and royal tennis. He jousted for twenty-six years. In his day, it was a bit safer than it had been in earlier times. The armour was heavier, and had a strong visor. The lances were brittle, and it was a sign of good jousting if you could get one to splinter on your opponent.

He liked to joust with his cousin, the Duke of Suffolk. In one bout in 1517, they broke eight lances each. In 1524, he forgot to close his visor and was nearly killed when a lance glanced the side of his helmet. This may have been the cause of the headaches Henry suffered in later life. In 1536, Henry was thrown from his heavily mailed horse which fell on top of him. He was knocked out for over two hours.

Other posh sports were hawking, hunting deer and riding at a ring with a lance.

BLOOD SPORTS

The tough Tudors loved blood and excitement. Cruelty was partly what made sport fun. Of course, there were those who tried to put an end to the blood, just as there are people who want to stop boxing today.

SPORTS REPORT: COCKFIGHTING

Here's an actual description of a cruel Tudor cockfight.

In the city of London, cock-fights are held annually throughout three-quarters of the year and I saw the place which is built like a theatre. The cocks are teased and incited to fly at one another, while those with wagers as to which cock will win sit closest. The spectators sit around higher up, watching with eager pleasure the fierce and angry fight between the cocks, as these wound each other to death with spurs and beaks.

31

SPORTS REPORT: BEAR BAITING

Read this horrible story of a Tudor bear-baiting session.

BAITING BEARS

In the middle of this place a large bear on a long rope was bound to a stake, then a number of great English mastiffs were brought in and shown first to the bear which they afterwards baited one after another. Although they were much struck and mauled by the bear, they did not give in, but had to be pulled off by sheer force. The bear's teeth were not sharp so they could not injure the dogs; they have them broken short.

The second bear was very big and old, and kept the dogs at bay so artfully with his paws that they could not score a point off him until there were more of them. When this bear was tired, a large white powerful bull was brought in, and likewise bound in the centre of the theatre, and one dog only was set on him at a time, which he speared with his horns, and tossed in such masterly fashion that they could not get the better of him.

Lastly they brought in an old blind bear which the boys hit with canes and sticks; but he knew how to untie his leash and he ran back to his stall.

SPORTS REPORT: FOOTBALL

There's nothing new about football hooligans – read this for the real-life details. The hooligans were the players!

> It may rather be called a friendly kind of fight than a play or recreation; a bloody and murdering practice, than a fellowly sport or pastime. Does not everyone lie in wait for his adversary, seeking to overthrow him, and to punch him on the nose, though it be on hard stones, in ditch or dale, in valley or hill, or what place it so ever it be, he cares not, so he may have him down? Sometimes their necks are broken, sometimes their backs, sometimes their legs, sometimes their arms, sometimes their noses gush out with blood, sometimes their eyes start out.

The two sides used to try to take the ball back to their villages, two or three miles apart. There were no rules and so many people got hurt that it was banned.

SPORTS REPORT: STOOL BALL

This was early cricket. A bundle of rags was used for the ball and the the 'wickets' were two posts about four metres apart. A stick was used for a bat. It's still played in parts of England.

SPORTS REPORT: THE MAYPOLE

Here's an actual description of this favourite Tudor knees-up.

> Every parish, town and village assemble themselves together, both men, women, and children, old and young; where they spend all the night in pleasant pastimes, and in the morning they return, bringing with them birch, boughs and branches of trees, to deck their assemblies.

> But their chiefest jewel they bring is their maypole, which is covered all over with flowers and herbs, bound round about with strings, from the top to the bottom, and sometimes painted with various colours, with two or three hundred men, women and children following it with great devotion.

> Then they start to banquet and feast, and leap and dance.

The Mayday festival goes back to Roman times. Activities included archery, morris dancing, choosing a May Queen and lighting bonfires.

HENRY GOES TO WORK

THE THREE YOUNG DUDES

Henry wanted to be a top king. So he had to show off to the other kings. The top cats in Europe at that time were three young dudes: Henry VIII himself, Francis I of France, and Charles V of the Holy Roman Empire.

DUDE 1

Henry's court was the most splendid, musical, intellectual and dynamic.

DUDE 2

Francis of France tried to be a splendid prince just like Henry. The French court was a bit ahead when it came to art and flirting. On the other hand, Francis had a long nose, and syphilis , although this didn't stop him chuckling over Henry's marriage problems.

DUDE 3

Charles V had a tricky job. The Holy Roman Empire was neither Holy, nor Roman nor an Empire. It was a collection of small German states. He was also King of Spain. His total Empire was so big and bitty it was hard keeping it together.

Syphilis is a sexually transmitted disease which was brought back to Europe from America by the sailors of Christopher Columbus in 1492.

To show off for England, Henry put on the greatest show on earth, 'The Field of the Cloth of Gold'. This was a grand tournament that was meant to bring peace and understanding between England and France. In fact it was more of a competition between Henry and Francis I of France to see who was the most stylish. The two kings met for a few days near Calais, each camping in gorgeous tents. One tent was made of gold cloth, thus giving the occasion its name. At the big moment they rode down opposite sides of a valley and embraced on horseback. Henry was wearing silver and gold, as was his horse. Francis was also in his best gear.

After this there was much jousting and feasting. The two kings were not allowed to fight, but Henry did have a go at wrestling with Francis and (so embarrassing) he lost. The English claimed that the French King had won by cheating. The whole thing was pointless and very expensive. Altogether, five thousand English people went across for a month, and with free wine flowing for all from fountains it was quite a party. In the middle of it all, Henry nipped back to England to talk to Francis' great enemy, the Emperor Charles.

WOLSEY –
THE SHOW-OFF

The young Henry didn't like the boring details of government, so he let Cardinal Wolsey take care of them. A butcher's son from Ipswich, Wolsey was ultra-efficient and soon Henry couldn't manage without him. Wolsey loved pomp and power and even wanted to be Pope. He was just the man to plan the Field of the Cloth of Gold.

Wolsey's only problem was that he was a bit too fond of money and he like to show off as well, sometimes putting Henry in the shade. Wolsey...

> would go out all in red in the clothes of a cardinal, which was either fine scarlet or crimson satin, the best he could get for money. On his head he had a round hat with a neck-piece of black velvet, holding in his hand a very fair orange, whereof the meat was taken out and fill up again with part of a sponge in which was vineger and other confections against diseased airs which he usually smelt when passing through a crowd.

Wolsey collected jobs, titles, money and houses like a squirrel collects nuts. He felt he deserved it. And Henry needed him – didn't he ?

BIG BOATS

The first thing Henry did as king with Wolsey's help was to build a big navy. These are the five biggest ships he took to war in 1513:

NAME	TON	SOLDIERS	SAILORS	GUNNERS
GREAT HARRY	1000	400	260	40
GABRIEL ROYAL	700	350	230	20
KATERYN FORTILEZA	700	300	210	40
SOVEREIGN	600	400	260	40
MARY ROSE	500	200	180	20

THE LOSS OF THE MARY ROSE

In 1545, the French were preparing to invade England. Henry assembled eighty ships. The French appeared off Portsmouth and the Mary Rose headed to meet them. The French were in retreat, so the Mary Rose turned to go back to harbour. As she turned, she capsized and lost nearly all of her crew of five hundred.

Henry tried to raise the ship three times. She was finally raised over four hundred years later in 1982 and you can go and see large chunks of the ship in Portsmouth.

AN ARMY MARCHES ON ITS BEER BELLY

A strong navy wasn't the only thing Henry felt he needed. Soldiers were also important in the king business. It's odd how often beer is mentioned in accounts of Tudor armies.

English soldiers liked their beer, and keeping them supplied was a tricky problem. When in 1512 Henry sent an army of 7,000 to help Spain against France, the lads were upset to find that the Spanish only served wine and cider. So they mutinied and Henry had to bring them home.

Henry attacked Scotland again in 1542. The invasion had to be held up in the north of England for nine days – because the beer hadn't arrived. When it did arrive, there was only enough for four days, so the Duke of Norfolk had to pull back earlier than planned. The Scots thought the English were running away and rashly attacked. They got caught in the bog at Solway Moss and were badly beaten.

In 1544, Henry sent Edward Seymour, to destroy Edinburgh. Seymour's problem was that he couldn't carry enough beer for his army across the mossy southern part of Scotland. He sent 16,000 men with their beer by sea in 114 ships. It worked! After a short march of fifteen miles, and three days' fighting, every building in Edinburgh, except for the Castle on its high rock, was burned to the ground.

In Henry's time beer began to take over from ale as the English drink. It was the same stuff really, although beer was flavoured with hops. Some Tudors feared the worst:

> And now of late days, it is much used in England to the detriment of many English men; specially it kills those who are troubled with colic, and the stone, and the strangulation; for the drink is a cold drink; yet it doth make a man fat and doth inflate the belly.

BEER FACT

During Henry VIII's reign, a number of consumer protection laws were passed. These were designed to force tradesmen to keep honest standards. They were much needed, if we believe this poem about an inn-keeper by Henry's tutor, John Skelton. Her name was Elynour Rumming, from Leatherhead. To make beer, she...

> Skimmeth it into a tray
> Where the yeast is
> With her maungy fystis:
> And sometimes she blends
> The dung of her hens
> And this ale
> together.

MONEY, MONEY, MONEY

The downside of being king was the cost of it all. Henry thought big and he had big bills to pay – for weapons, soldiers, ships, tournaments, fancy clothes and big feasts...

He...
Grabbed land from traitors,
Raised taxes,
Asked for presents.

But none of it was enough. The French wars and the feasts played havoc with Henry's piggy bank. Things looked really dire when suddenly he had a brilliant idea – close down the monasteries and grab their wealth! It was brilliantly simple and it tied in with a couple of other things which were bothering him. Read on...

GO HOME, ROME

HOLY HENRY

Henry was a Roman Catholic when he started out. Things began to go wrong between Henry and the Pope, the head of the Roman Catholics, because Henry wanted a son to inherit his throne, but poor Catherine couldn't produce a boy baby.

Henry started to look elsewhere and he soon fell in love with a woman called Anne Boleyn. The trouble was, Catherine wouldn't agree to a divorce and the Pope wouldn't give one. Even Mr Fix-It, Cardinal Wolsey, failed to persuade him.

Well, the Pope was Head of the Church. If he wouldn't grant Henry a divorce from Catherine of Aragon, then the Church in England would be divorced from the Pope! Henry would head the Church himself. So it was goodbye Cardinal Wolsey and hello, Thomas Cranmer and Thomas Cromwell. Cranmer was a shrewd clergyman with new Protestant ideas. Cromwell was a smart fixer in the Wolsey mode.

It took them about six years to split England from Rome and free Henry to marry Anne Boleyn.

SPOT THE PROT

Wolsey was a Catholic. Cranmer was a Protestant. Some of these statements are made by Protestants and some by Roman Catholics. Can you tell which is which?

1 I believe that no priest or bishop can stand between me and God.

2 I believe the actual body of Christ is in the communion bread.

3 I believe that I can get rid of my sins by confessing them and doing penance.

4 I believe that the Pope is the head of the church.

5 I believe the Pope is a greedy foreigner.

6 I don't like incense and religious paintings.

ANSWERS:

5) Protestant
6) Protestant

3) Catholic
4) Catholic

1) Protestant
2) Catholic

44

MONKEY BUSINESS

The change in the Church which Henry started was
not just because of his own love life and lack of
money. The Roman Catholic Church was unpopular.
Many leading churchmen, like Cardinal Wolsey, held
well-paid jobs without doing much. The Church
played on people's superstitions, and fear of what
would happen when they died. One monastery kept
these holy relics:

✞ the coals that Saint Laurence was once toasted
   with;

✞ a clipping from Saint Edmund's nails;

✞ the pen-knife and boots of Saint Thomas of
   Canterbury;

✞ different holy skulls for curing the headache;

✞ enough pieces of the Holy Cross to make a whole
   cross;

✞ other relics to make rain and kill weeds.

Some monks were slack and lived pretty well. They
had their own special laws, which seemed unfair for
other people. Monks could not marry, but they
sometimes lived with women anyway. The fact that
they taxed people on their lands did not make them
any more popular.

As well as all the ornaments, relics and paintings,
which the new Protestants thought were a load of
hooey, the Church owned a quarter of England.

MESSING UP THE MONASTERIES

The break with Rome took just six years. Here's the timetable:

1533   Henry gets Parliament to make him Head of the Church

1534   Parliament forces clergy to obey Henry

1535   Grand Survey of monasteries' wealth

1536-40   Government overhaul, and tax collection

1536   Dissolution of smaller monasteries (and grabbing their wealth)

1537-40   English bible in church and other reforms

1539   Dissolution of the large monasteries (and grabbing their wealth)

It was a huge windfall for Henry. Take a look at the accounts:

ACCOUNTS

RECEIVED

Revenue from monastery lands	£415,000
Sale of monastery lands	£855,711
Sale of buildings, bells, lead etc	£26,502
Sale of silver and gold plate	£79,081
	£1,376,294

PAID OUT

Pensions to monks and nuns	£33,045
PROFIT	£1,343,251

This was a vast sum in those days. From then on, whenever Henry was short of a bit of cash, he sold off some church land. This tied the new land-owners to the Protestant cause – after all, they didn't want Roman Catholics taking their land back.

WIFE STRIFE

WIFELY WOE IN TUDOR TIMES

Henry had so many wives, it gets confusing. Here are some rhymes to make it easy to remember.

Catherine, Anne and Jane;
Anne, Catherine, Catherine again.

There's another rhyme to remember
what happened to them:

Divorced, beheaded, died;
Divorced, beheaded, survived.

The divorces were really
annulments. An annulment
says that the marriage never happened
in the first place. Tough on Anne Boleyn and Catherine
Howard, who were beheaded for adultery –
during marriages which Henry later denied had
happened anyway!

So why did Henry keep getting married?

🔔   He wanted a male heir to keep the Tudors going.

🔔   It seemed like a neat diplomatic move at the time.

🔔   He wanted to be respectable.

   This was a problem for Henry. Nearly all the women in England of the right breeding, were cousins of his. Or they were cousins of someone he'd already married, or they'd already married his brother.

PARENTS: the most Catholic King and Queen of Spain.

PERSONALITY: loyal, brave, long-suffering.

LENGTH OF MARRIAGE: twenty-four years.

PROBLEM: couldn't produce a healthy baby boy to become the next Tudor king.

CHILDREN: a girl, Mary, later Bloody Queen Mary.

OTHER PROBLEMS: after Henry had fallen in love with Anne Boleyn, Catherine was too high-born to behead. She bravely stuck to her guns and refused a divorce.

RESULT: after England's break with Rome, a divorce went through and then an annulment, a bit of a joke after twenty-four years! Catherine was shunted off to live in the country, where she died in 1536.

WIFE NO 2: ANNE BOLEYN

PARENTS: the ambitious Protestant Sir Thomas Boleyn, and the Duke of Norfolk's sister Elizabeth.

PERSONALITY: ambitious, vain and intelligent. Not very good-looking and had a kind of sixth finger on one hand, which she tried to hide. Also rumoured to have three breasts! Classy with lots of style, but not much liked.

LENGTH OF MARRIAGE: three years (plus long courtship waiting for the divorce from Catherine of Aragon to come through).

CHILDREN: a girl, Elizabeth, later Good Queen Bess.

PROBLEM: couldn't produce a healthy baby boy to become the next Tudor king. All sorts of evidence was dug up to show that Anne was having lots of affairs with with young courtiers.

RESULT: divorce, execution in 1536, annulment.

WIFE NO 3: JANE SEYMOUR

PARENTS: the Seymours were Protestant (her brother Edward became her son's protector as Duke of Northumberland.)

PERSONALITY: plain, friendly, modest, virtuous. Just the ticket. She was the one Henry wanted to be buried with at the end.

LENGTH OF MARRIAGE: one year. (They were secretly engaged on the day after Anne Boleyn was beheaded.)

PROBLEM: she died after giving birth.

CHILDREN: a boy! He grew up to be Edward VI, the Boy King.

PARENTS: powerful German Protestant prince, John of Cleves, and his wife.

PERSONALITY: cheerful, stolid, simple.

LENGTH OF MARRIAGE: about 6 months.

PROBLEM: Henry found her unattractive, nothing like her portrait, and he fancied Catherine Howard.

CHILDREN: none.

SOLUTION: friendly divorce in 1548. Retired to the country. Survived Henry by ten years. Henry blamed Cromwell for this mistaken marriage, and had him executed. Anne died in 1557.

THE WRONG CHOICE

Before Anne came to England, Henry had only seen a portrait of her.

When she arrived, he wanted to get an early look at her, so he pretended to be someone bringing a gift from the king. When Anne realised that this huge man was the King of England himself, she didn't have enough English to talk to him. Henry left, still hanging on to the present he had brought her.

Henry was disappointed. He is said to have called her 'a Flanders mare'. They shared a bed for a few nights only. It seemed that Anne was plain, scared of Henry's vast hulk, and didn't know anything about sex.

When the ladies of the Queen's bedchamber said they hoped that she was pregnant, she told them, "When he comes to bed he kisses me and taketh me by the hand and biddeth me 'Good night, Sweet Heart' and in the morning biddeth me 'Farewell, darling'. Is not this enough?" By the spring Henry was flirting with Catherine Howard. Anne of Cleves was helpful about the divorce and stayed friendly with Henry in a sisterly way. Her brother the Duke of Cleves was "glad his sister had fared no worse".

WIFE NO 5: CATHERINE HOWARD

PARENTS: the Catholic Duke of Norfolk's brother and Joyce Culpepper.

PERSONALITY: young, beautiful, small, lively, a Catholic. Henry at first thought her 'a blushing rose without a thorn'.

LENGTH OF MARRIAGE: a year and a bit.

PROBLEM: jealousy. The Protestants dug up a lot of rumours about Catherine. When she had lived at her aunt's, a sort of posh finishing school for well-born young ladies, some young men may have visited the dormitories. Some said she was still having other lovers. Henry lost his temper when he heard the rumours. He yelled for a sword, and burst into tears.

CHILDREN: none.

RESULT: heads off for Catherine and her supposed lovers in 1542.

PARENTS: daughter of Sir Thomas Parr of Kendal.

PERSONALITY: intelligent and religious. Already married twice. Had brought up children successfully.

LENGTH OF MARRIAGE: four years. She was Henry's last wife and survived him. Henry was very decrepit when he was old, and Catherine was really a kind of nanny to him and his three children.

PROBLEMS: none to speak of.

CHILDREN: none of Henry's.

RESULT: outlived Henry but only by a year. She managed one more marriage before she died in 1548.

HEADS AND TAILS

Can you match these heads of Henry's wives with the dates and manner of their deaths?

HAL'S OTHER GALS

Have a peep at Hal's private diary...

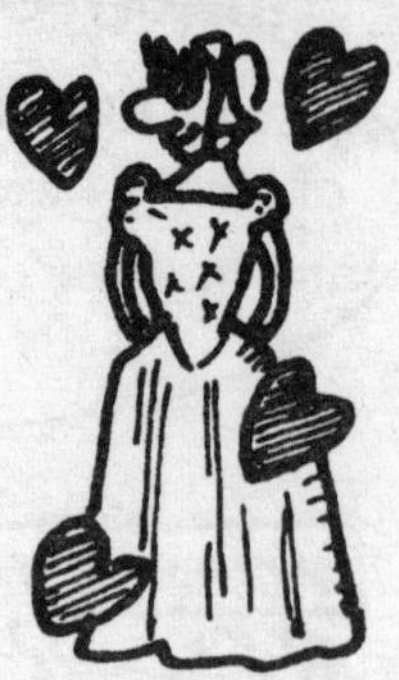

1510 Catherine pregnant. I don't half fancy that Anne Hastings. This evening I sent a messenger, but that Fool her brother the Duke of Buckingham Says he'll send Anne away from Court to a convent if I get near her. Buckingham had better watch out, also he has a claim to the throne, so im going to watch him closely!

1514 That Jane Popyngcort is a corker. She been mistress of the Duke de Longueville, m prisoner of war. She was supposed to go to France with the Duke and my sister Mary, who's to marry the French King Louis XII. But Louis has refused to let in Popyngcort – because of her evil life. What an idiot!

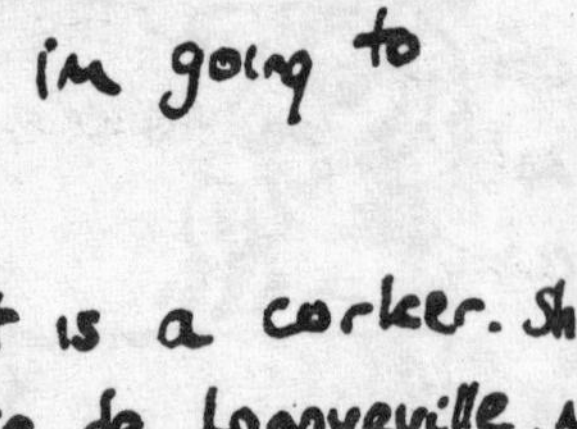

Anyway with the Duke

out of the way, this is my chance of popping into bed with Popyngcart myself. Goody.

1525 I shall have to finish my affair with Mary Boleyn. She certainly learned a thing or two at the French Court! Although it was rude of the French King to call her a Hackney – a horse that is hired out. I shall marry her off to a courtier and pass my children off as her husband's. Her sister Anne's not bad looking either come to think about it.

1535 Madge Skelton is being dangled in front of my eyes by those rascally Norfolks – anything to keep themselves in favour now that I'm fed up with Anne Boleyn. I know when I'm being used. Norfolk had better <u>watch out</u>.

HENRY'S SISTERS

Henry's sisters both had plenty of tough Tudor spirit.

MARGARET, QUEEN OF SCOTS

Margaret was married to the dashing James IV of Scotland in 1503, but he was slaughtered at Flodden Field in 1513 by her brother Henry's army. She fled to England for a while but returned to Scotland where she married again. Her grandchild, James VI of Scotland, later became James I of England.

MARY, QUEEN OF FRANCE

Mary was first engaged to Emperor Charles V but nothing came of it. She fell in love with the Duke of Suffolk, but Henry married her off to the old dotard King Louis XII of France. The wedding took place – at long distance – before Mary even left England. She had to get into bed, while the Duc de Longueville, the French King's stand-in, "with one leg naked from the middle of the thigh downwards, went into bed and touched the Princess with his bared foot". The real Louis XII died soon enough. She then secretly married Suffolk.

IMAGINE I'M DOTTY OLD LOUIS.

I'D RATHER NOT.

WOMEN'S PAGE

Not all Tudor women wore fancy clothes, flirted with the king or got their heads chopped off. Most of them had to work. Common women married much later than noblewomen – twenty-five was quite a normal age.

Once married, there was plenty to do. Most people lived on the land.

A farmer's wife had to:
1 Pray when getting out of bed
2 Clean the house
3 Lay the table
4 Milk the cows
5 Dress the children
6 Cook all meals
7 Brew the beer
8 Bake the bread
9 Send corn to the mill
10 Make butter and cheese
11 Mind the swine (the pigs not her husband)
12 Collect the eggs

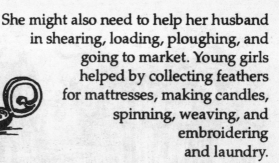

She might also need to help her husband in shearing, loading, ploughing, and going to market. Young girls helped by collecting feathers for mattresses, making candles, spinning, weaving, and embroidering and laundry.

COUNTRY CLOTHES

Poor people wore rough woollen clothes.

Young girls were not allowed to wear hats as hats meant that a person was important. When they were married, they could wear a hat. One law stated that they had to wear a hat made of English wool.

To keep long skirts out of the deep mud, country women wore platform shoes. These either had thick wooden soles or were kept off the ground by iron rings.

In Henry's time, the women dressed quite plainly. Later when Elizabeth came to the throne, everyone dressed more smartly. Girls aimed to have fair hair, pale skin, red lips and blue eyes.

But whatever else they did, they avoided having too many baths. Baths were thought to be bad for you, although Queen Elizabeth prided herself on her cleanliness – she had a bath every three months.

Ordinary English women were mostly freer than other women of their time. They got married late, and often had a lot of responsibility within the household. English women spoke their minds. Many of the Protestant martyrs, like Anne Askew, were outspoken and brave women.

One visitor from Italy thought that English wives were not as pure as they should be. He said that many of them had lovers, but were very careful to keep them secret. The Italians also thought English women were very beautiful, and liked the way English men and women kissed whenever they met.

He noticed that English men were always shaking hands with each other.

FEMALE PUNISHMENTS

Despite some freedom, life could be very tough for Tudor women. They were never really thought of as adults and, unless they were widows, they were always under the control of either husbands or fathers. Men had several ways of keeping women down.

Nagging or scolding was a crime. The first time, a woman accused of it might be warned in church. The second time, she would be for the ducking-stool. The woman was tied to a chair at the end of a pole that rested on a pivot, and lowered into the water. It was horrible. Some women drowned.

The third time, she would get the 'brakes'. This was an iron mask that fitted on to the head, with a metal bar going into the woman's mouth to hold her tongue down. It was very uncomfortable and painful.

WITCHCRAFT

One of the nastiest ways to get at someone was to accuse them of being a witch. Often the victim was a lonely old woman, or a herbal healer.

It was thought that Satan (the Devil) gave some people special powers which they used through familiars. These familiars were creatures that were animal or spirit or both.

People were ignorant. It was easy to think that someone was getting at you by evil magic. If a woman was accused, it was very hard for her to prove her innocence.

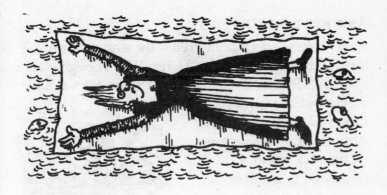

One strange test was to put the accused woman into a sack or onto a sheet and lay her on the water. If she sank, she was innocent (because she was pure the water had accepted her). Too bad if she also drowned!

It was in Henry VIII's time that witchcraft became a crime. In the following century, you could be executed for it.

HARD BIRTHS

Women could only stop work for a short while to have babies. This was a risky business for mother and child. In Tudor times, only one baby in ten would live to the age of forty. About half of the babies would die in their first year, and many women, like Jane Seymour, would die in or just after childbirth.

AND HARD DEATHS

Anne Askew was a keen Protestant who gave out leaflets during the reign of Henry VIII. Though Henry split with Rome he remained a Catholic – it was still dangerous to express Protestant religious ideas. Anne Askew was tortured on the rack and sentenced to death by burning. Despite the torture, she never betrayed anyone, but her legs were so badly injured she had to be carried to the place of execution in a chair. She wrote a moving account of her torture. A high number of Protestant martyrs were women.

The rack was an instrument to stretch arms and legs. The victim was tied at hands and wrists and pulled slowly apart. It caused horrible pain.

YES, MINISTERS

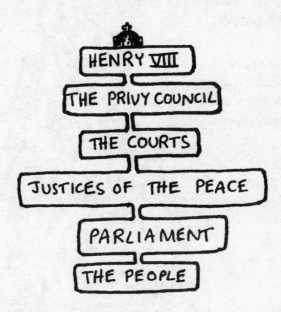

THE POWER TOWER

HENRY VIII

THE PRIVY COUNCIL

THE COURTS

JUSTICES OF THE PEACE

PARLIAMENT

THE PEOPLE

England had a small population, so it was easy for Henry to rule it, and even easier after he had made himself Head of the Church and got rid of the monasteries and the authority of the Pope. Although Henry was a tough Tudor tyrant, his power was not unlimited. He needed Parliament to approve laws and raise money. Regional councils were set up for the fringes of England which were hard to manage from the centre, and full of unruly Celts.

TUDOR ENGLAND
THE SHAPE OF HENRY'S KINGDOM

TOWNS
London had only 60,000 people which makes it about the same size as a market town today. No other town had more than 10,000 people.

POPULATION
2,600,000 – about twice the size of Birmingham.

INDUSTRY
Not much. Quite a lot of wool shipped to Europe.

TRAVEL
Some roads for horses and lumbering carriages. But mud often made land travel very hard. Most journeys by foot or by river.

THREE KINDS OF MINISTER

Henry had three kinds of minister – thinkers, fixers and soldiers.

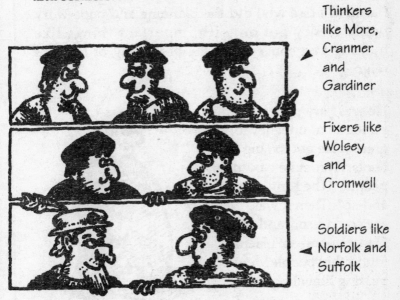

Thinkers like More, Cranmer and Gardiner

Fixers like Wolsey and Cromwell

Soldiers like Norfolk and Suffolk

At the beginning of his reign, while still a good Roman Catholic, Henry relied on Wolsey and More to run things while he himself had fun. Later, Henry handled things himself more and more.

After the problem of the divorce from Catherine of Aragon and the break with Rome, Henry got Cromwell to run things, following Cranmer's advice.

Right at the end of his reign, Henry got rid of the conservatives, Gardiner and the Duke of Norfolk, to leave a smooth path for his son Edward VI, and new Protestant leaders like Somerset and Northumberland.

CARDINAL WOLSEY, FIXER
c. 1475-1530

We've already met Wolsey, the fat cat with the Cardinal's hat, who did the planning and paperwork while Henry got on with important things like hunting and concerts, at the beginning of Henry's reign.

He was very clever and fair-minded but unbelievably greedy. He got too big for his boots. At first he would tell people, "The King says so-and-so". Then it was, "We say so-and-so," and finally, "I say so-and-so". Henry found that people were by-passing him altogether.

Wolsey amassed loadsa money, loadsa jobs and loadsa houses. He built palaces at Hampton Court and Whitehall much more lavish than anything Henry had. But as a jumped-up monk, he made enemies of the old-guard nobility. Anne Boleyn hated him anyway because he had once stopped her marrying her first love.

Finally when Henry called him to London to be tried for treason, Wolsey, with his usual foresight, died before he could get there.

SIR THOMAS MORE, THINKER
1478-1535

More was ultra-clever. He wrote a clever satire called "Utopia" and became Henry's main advisor. Although he sniped at the Roman Catholic Church, he would have nothing to do with Protestantism. He persecuted Protestants vigorously on Henry's behalf.

More's son-in-law, William Roper, once told More how lucky he was to be a friend of the King. More replied:

> I find his grace my very good lord indeed, and I believe he does as much favour me as any other subject in this realm. However, son Roper, I may tell you I have no cause to be proud of it. For, if my head could win him a castle in France, it should not fail to go.

But Henry knew More would not recognise him as Head of the Church. He died on the chopping block.

THOMAS CRANMER, THINKER
1489-1556

Cranmer was a cautious clergyman, one of a bunch of churchmen who used to meet in a Cambridge pub. Henry was interested in his ideas and called him to court to

TIME FOR ANOTHER?

sort out the divorce from Catherine of Aragon and to set up Henry as the head of the Church of England.

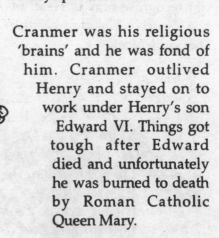

Cranmer shaped the Church of England and wrote the Prayer Book. He was hated by Roman Catholics and the aristocrats, but Henry always protected him.

Cranmer was his religious 'brains' and he was fond of him. Cranmer outlived Henry and stayed on to work under Henry's son Edward VI. Things got tough after Edward died and unfortunately he was burned to death by Roman Catholic Queen Mary.

KING HENRY SAVES CRANMER

The Duke of Norfolk and Gardiner wanted to get rid of Cranmer. They didn't like his church reforms or his influence over Henry. Charges were drawn up against him. If he was found guilty he would die. So Henry called at Lambeth Palace in his barge and made sure that Cranmer was in charge of the investigation against himself. Cranmer found himself not guilty.

Two years later, Norfolk again tried to arrest Cranmer, this time at the Council table. Henry again warned Cranmer, and gave Cranmer his ring. All Cranmer had to do was to show this ring to his accusers to win the right of personal appeal to the King. Norfolk spoke against Cranmer in Council and was amazed when Cranmer produced the King's ring. Henry then ticked off Norfolk and his allies. However Cranmer was no longer able to benefit from the king's protection after Henry and his son Edward VI had died.

THOMAS CROMWELL, FIXER
1599-1658

Cromwell was a Jack-of-all-trades from Putney. His father may have been a clothworker, an alehouse keeper or a blacksmith. Young Thomas got into trouble as a young man and left England to work as a soldier and a merchant in Europe.

Henry brought Cromwell in to help him fix the divorce from Catherine of Aragon. He closed down the monasteries and fixed the downfall of Anne Boleyn. He was hated by Catholics and by the old guard nobility. To them he was an upstart. His big mistake was to have the idea that Henry should marry Anne of Cleves. His enemies then accused him of being too big for his boots and a Protestant. Henry chose to believe them.

Cromwell wrote a letter to the King which ended, "I cry for mercy, mercy, mercy," but it was no use. He was beheaded.

CHARLES BRANDON, DUKE OF SUFFOLK, SOLDIER 1484-1545

Big and bluff, he was Henry's jousting partner. His one big mistake was to run off with Henry's sister Mary after her first husband, the decrepit King Louis XII of France, had died. They married secretly.

Although Henry fined him so severely he was never able to pay the fine off, Henry forgave his old mate. Suffolk was ever loyal and ever reliable, one of the great survivors in Henry's court.

EDWARD GARDINER, BISHOP OF WINCHESTER FIXER c.1490-1555

Gardiner was a clever clergyman of the Wolsey type. He liked persecuting Protestants if Henry would let him. The Bishop of Winchester, described him with these words: "a swart colour, a hanging look, frowning brows, deep-set eyes, a nose hooked like a buzzard, great paws (like the devil), an outward monster with a vengeable wit."

A CHOP ON THE OLD BLOCK!

TREASON AND OTHER CRIMES

Being put in the Tower of London was a dramatic experience. You knew you were part of history. Of course, your feelings would depend largely on whether you were going to be executed or not. So many important people went to the Tower that it became a matter of pride for their descendants.

In Henry's time, the Tower was not a lonely place. It was really busy, because the Tower was an all purpose building – it was a palace, a prison, a fortress, an armoury, a mint (for making coins), a treasure house and a zoo.

Important prisoners might be allowed to live quite well, in spacious rooms, receiving visitors and going out for walks in the Tower grounds. It was a great place to study and get some writing done. Torture was not supposed to happen, but it did. It was not a punishment, just a way of getting evidence!

Many prisoners left engraved pictures and poems on the walls of the prison. You can see these, as well as

Henry VIII's armour and
weapons, in the Tower of
London today. The Yeoman
of the Guard still guard the
Tower and dress in Tudor
costume. They are called
Beefeaters. An 'eater' was
another word for a servant,
someone who ate at the
Lord's expense.

OFF WITH HIS HEAD

The Tower of London was a busy place. Aristocrats
were generally beheaded there. Ordinary traitors
were hung, drawn and quartered elsewhere.

See how busy they were in the Tower:

1509   CHOP! Empson and Dudley, his dad's tax
       collectors.
1521   CHOP! Duke of Buckingham.
1535   CHOP! Bishop Fisher.
       CHOP! Sir Thomas More.
1536   SWISH! Anne Boleyn.
1538   CHOP! The Pole family.
1540   CHOP! Thomas Cromwell.
1542   CHOP! Catherine Howard.
1547   CHOP! Earl of Surrey.
1552   SWING! Duke of Somerset.
1554   BANG! Seven die in gunpowder explosion.
       CHOP! CHOP! CHOP! CHOP! Lady Jane Grey,
       Guildford Dudley, Duke of Northumberland,
       Sir Thomas Wyatt.

WHAT WAS IT LIKE TO BE BEHEADED?

Beheading was a punishment reserved for important traitors (small fry were hung, drawn and quartered - disembowelled while still alive). If you were going to be beheaded it was important to put on a good show for the crowd. First you made your peace with God – as you were shortly going to meet him and be judged this was important. On the platform it was a good idea to make a speech saying how right the King was to execute you. This could save your family. Being nice to the axeman was also advised, so he would make a clean job of it. Finally it was important to be brave and composed about the whole affair.

COULD YOU TRY THE AXE FIRST?

The axe was a pretty heavy instrument and when if fell on someone's neck, the head tended to bounce up in the air. That's why the chopping block came to be shaped with a space for the face to fit in. When the axe came down, the head just rolled away. It was quite a skill to take off someone's head with one blow. Sometimes it took several, and the executioner might have to finish the job with a saw.

LAST WORDS

People about to be executed were often brave and witty. The Lieutenant of the Tower told More he was sorry that it wasn't more comfortable in the Tower. More said he wasn't complaining, but if he should complain, the Lieutenant could throw him out. When he was to be executed, More was weak and had trouble climbing the scaffold, so he appealed for help: "I pray you, Master Lieutenant, to see me safe up. For my coming down, let me shift for myself." Then he said to the executioner: "Pluck up thy spirits, man, and be not afraid: my neck is very short."

The night before Anne Boleyn was to be executed, she put her hands around her neck and told the Lord Lieutenant of the Tower that as she had "so little a neck", the job of the executioner would not be hard. An expert swordsman was brought over from Calais as a special favour. It is said that her lips were still moving in prayer after the head was severed. The day before Catherine Howard was to be beheaded, she asked for the chopping block to be brought to her apartment so that she could rehearse, and so not fluff her performance. Lady Jane Grey, only sixteen, was calm and brave.

When she was blindfolded, she could not find the block and asked, "What shall I do? Where is it?" She was guided to it and her last words were a prayer.

LORD INTO THY HANDS I COMMEND MY SPIRIT.

SIR THOMAS HAS A LUCKY ESCAPE

Sir Thomas Knyvett had a lucky escape. He was found guilty of causing a fight at a tennis match at court. He was sentenced not only to lose his lands and goods but also his right hand. Many of the King's household were there to help out.

The sergeant surgeon brought his cutting instruments. The sergeant of the woodyard brought the mallet and the block. The master cook brought the knife. The sergeant of the larder came to position the knife. The sergeant farrier brought searing irons. The yeoman of the chandlery brought dressings. The yeoman of the scullery brought a pan of fire to heat the irons and a chafer of water to cool them. The yeoman of the ewery brought a basin, jug and towels. The sergeant of the poultry brought a live cock for practice.

Finally, Knyvett asked for a message to be taken to the King, asking if he could lose his left hand rather than the right because, "If my right hand be spared I may hereafter do much good service to his Grace as shall please him to appoint." Henry liked this message. He ordered the sentence to be lifted.

PHEW!

VILLAINS

Not everyone who was executed in Henry's England was innocent, or a minister, or a beautiful lady. There were plenty of real villains about as well. They had special Tudor tricks.

CUTPURSES

There were no pockets as such. People carried their money in small purses tied to the belt. The cutpurse would cut the ties and make off with your purse.

ANGLERS

These were thieves who used long poles with removable hooks on the end to grab valuables through the windows of houses.

RUFFLER

These were beggars with sob stories to tell to try to get people to give money.

ABRAM MAN

A beggar who pretended to be crazy.

PRIGGER

A horse thief.

DUMMERER

A beggar who acted deaf and dumb.

The Tudors had laws against almost everything, and punishments too. There were laws about how long you had to work and what clothes you could wear. There was a curfew to tell you when you had to be indoors at night. There was no police force. Citizens had to take it in turn to act as constables and patrol the streets.

FOREIGNERS

We've seen how Londoners were famous for hating foreigners in Henry's VII time. Nothing changed very much in Henry VIII's reign.

> They have such fierce tempers and wicked ideas they not only scorn the way in which Italians live, but actually chase them with uncontrolled hatred ... Here in the daytime they look at us with horror, and at night they sometimes drive us away with kicks, and blows of their sticks.

No nonsense about attracting tourists in those days! In 1497, a Venetian diplomat wrote about the English:

> They think there are no other men than themselves, and no other world but England. Whenever they see a handsome foreigner, they say 'he looks like an Englishman'.

In 1517, the 'Evil May Day Riots' broke out after a rumour that Italian merchants were after the wives and daughters of Englishmen. Henry put a number of the rioters to death. The anti-foreign feeling encouraged people to support Henry against the Pope. After all Popes were usually Italian.

SPITTING AND KISSING

Spitting was a popular way to show contempt and not just to foreigners. People sitting in the stocks as a punishment might be spat at. Women spat at men who got too friendly.

Once two Protestant clergyman were put in prison and sentenced to death. One of them was an extreme radical Arian (a religious sect) who did not believe that Jesus was the son of God. The other, Philpot, spat in the man's face when he discovered his shocking beliefs, and then quickly wrote a pamphlet called 'The Apology of John Philpot for Spitting Upon an Arian'!

On the other hand the English were also famous for kissing each other. When the Dutch scholar Erasmus visited England, he complained that whenever he went to a house he had to kiss everyone – including the cat!

STURDY BEGGARS

Lots of people were put to death during Henry's reign, most of them for theft. One Elizabethan thought that 72,000 had been put to death out of just three million people. A lot of the thefts were by vagabonds who had no other way of getting food. Vagabonds were unemployed men who travelled around getting a living any way they could. Sometimes they were people thrown out of the army or off monastery land. Punishing the sturdy beggars was a Tudor way of dealing with the problem. Lots of different punishments were used. Here are some of them.

BEATING
Henry VIII ordered that vagrants be tied to the end of a cart and beaten until bloody.

STOCKS AND PILLORY
The stocks was a sort of seat with holes to secure the feet. The pillory was a plank with holes for the head and hands.

REBELS AND SHEEP

THEY DARED TO SAY NO

In Tudor times, English trade in woollen cloth doubled. It sold like hot cakes all over Europe. To cash in on the profits, landlords fenced in large areas of common land for sheep to graze on.

For an ordinary labourer this was a disaster. It meant he had lost the common land that he had always been able to use. Also, as sheep didn't need much looking after there was less farm work around. No wonder there were so many filthy starving beggars stumbling round the countryside.

Sir Thomas More felt sorry for the poor. He wrote:

> Your sheep, which were so meek and tame and such small eaters, now, as I hear told, have become great devourers and so wild that they eat up and swallow men. They take over, destroy and devour whole fields, houses and towns. For, if you look in any part of the country that grows the finest and dearest wool, there you find noblemen and gentlemen, and even certain abbots (holy men without doubt) not content with the yearly income and profits of their ancestors have greatly abused the public interest.

WHOSE FAULT WAS IT?

We have figures for Leicestershire, which show who was enclosing the land.

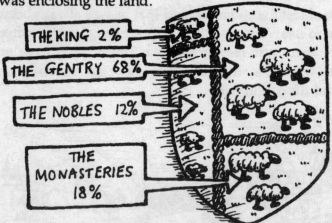

THE KING 2%

THE GENTRY 68%

THE NOBLES 12%

THE MONASTERIES 18%

The gentry were chiefly responsible for enclosing land – 68% of enclosed land fell into their hands. With the break-up of the monasteries, the process of enclosure would go even further. The system was turning labourers into beggars.

PILGRIMAGE OF GRACE? OR BLOODY REBELLION?

In 1536-7, a whole string of bloody rebellions, known as the Pilgrimage of Grace, erupted across the land. The rebels had many different reasons for rebelling. Some were against the smashing of the smaller monasteries. Some noble rebels hated the way the Tudors were reducing their power. Many rebels were worried about enclosures.

One of these rebellions was led by Robert Aske in Yorkshire. He was followed by 40,000 men. The Thames was low and the rebels could easily have crossed it and captured London. Henry pretended to talk. He invited the leaders to Greenwich and seemed to give in to their wishes and to pardon them. He gave Aske a crimson satin jacket.

But when the next bit of fighting broke out in Yorkshire, Henry arrested and executed all the rebels from the early uprisings as well. Henry ordered that all the captured rebels be hung, drawn and quartered and their heads and other bits be displayed all over the place, in towns great and small.

SIR ANTHONY'S SICK JOKE

After a similar uprising against the enclosures in Cornwall in 1549, Sir Anthony Kingston was sent by the government to punish the rebels. When he arrived at Bodmin, he was invited to dinner by the Mayor. Sir Anthony accepted but told the mayor to put up a scaffold in the courtyard as there would be some hangings after dinner.

After a good dinner, the mayor told Sir Anthony that the scaffold was now erected. Sir Anthony then told the Mayor to go up on the scaffold as he was one of those who were going to be hanged.

MEDIA MEGA-STARS

WHO WAS WHO ON THE EARLY TUDOR SCENE

MULTI-MEDIA

Media for Tudors meant music or writing and a bit of painting. Henry VIII loved music – and in his day English music was the tops in Europe. Henry himself could sing well, play lute, flute, organ and virginal (a keyboard instrument), and compose.

When dancing, gentlemen might try the stately pavane, the faster galliard or the exciting volta. In the volta, ladies were lifted in the air. The skills of muscians, artists, writers and dancers would all be needed for a top class 'revel'. Read on...

Join the Revel

Top musicians, artists and writers will all have the chance to show off at a tournament at Westminster on 12th and 15th February, 1511. For your enjoyment we are proud to present the following attractions:

- ♦ a pageant car decorated as a forest with rocks, hills, and dales and a golden castle in the middle

- ● a pantomime lion and antelope

- ♦ an interlude of music praising the infant prince

- ● a dance led by six couples

Special guest appearance by King Henry himself!

TEN TOP TUDORS

No 1 – ROBERT FAYREFAX 1464–1521

Robert was top musician at Henry's court in the
1520s. Henry paid good money to his musicians and
Fairfax lived well. He had his own choir and they
sang in tune – unlike the choir at the French court
who could neither sing in time nor tune, and where
the chief singing master
was mostly drunk.

As a sideline
Fayrefax
copied out
music,
charging
£20 for a
prick-song
book. Henry
gave him a big
funeral in St Alban's
Abbey when he died.

No 2 – MEMMO

Friar Denis Memmo was a Venetian organist who
moved to England in 1516. People could listen to him
for hours on end, he was so good at playing. In fact
he was so good that he asked for more money in a
song which he wrote. As Henry grew more brutal
Memmo fled England and ended up living in
Portugal.

 A prick-song book was one in which the notes were written, or 'pricked'
onto the paper.

No 3 – HENRY VIII OF ENGLAND 1491-1547

Yes, Henry himself was a great musician. He had a good voice and played several instruments. He may have written 'Greensleeves', the Tudor chart-topper.

No 4 – SIR THOMAS MALORY D.1471

A failed highwayman and soldier, Sir Thomas Malory wrote his best work while rotting in prison around 1469. 'Morte d'Arthur' (the death of King Arthur) shot to the top of the Tudor pops and was a big hit all over Europe. Sir Thomas's version of King Arthur is grim and bloody. The Tudors liked the story of King Arthur, because Arthur was a Welshman like Henry VII, and his story helped their own claim to the

throne of England. In 'Morte d'Arthur', Arthur is betrayed by his wife Guinevere and his close friend Sir Lancelot, who have an affair together. Malory got his Arthur stories from older French versions of the story.

No 5- JOHN HEYWOOD

There wasn't much in the way of English theatre before Shakespeare's time. Ordinary people had to make do with the odd morality play or the occasional medieval mystery story.

At court, however, there was a new thing called an interlude. This was a short play in English. John Heywood was top of the interlude writers. He was a minstrel under Henry VIII and then court jester under Edward VI and Mary. As a Catholic, he chose to leave the country when Elizabeth became Queen. Heywood, ministrel and jester, was a trailblazer for the Elizabethan greats, Shakespeare, Marlowe and Jonson. He died in Belgium.

ANYONE FOR AN INTERLUDE?

Diplomat and courtier, Sir Thomas Wyatt was number one Tudor poet during Henry's reign. He may also have been Anne Boleyn's lover before she caught Henry's eye. By Henry's time poetry was not what it had been in the great days of the fourteenth century. John Skelton, Henry's tutor, wrote some funny verses, but no one produced good love poetry.

What was wanted was something smoother, like the Italian Petrarch's sonnets. Sonnets were just fourteen lines long, and they had to be clever to please fashionable Tudor noblemen. It wasn't easy at first. English was a rougher language than Italian and making it rhyme is harder because we don't have lots of words ending in 'a' like the Italians do.

Sir Thomas cracked it and thus helped to start a whole new fashion. Soon everyone was writing sonnets.

ANNE'S LOCKET

The story goes that Sir Thomas Wyatt playfully stole Anne Boleyn's locket in the same week that Henry took a ring of hers which he then wore on his finger. Henry and Wyatt played bowls together.

Henry pointed to the bowls with the finger which wore Anne's ring, and said, pointedly, "I tell thee it is mine," meaning not the game, but the ring and Anne.

Wyatt asked if he could measure the distances between the bowls. (In the game of bowls the player whose ball is nearest to a smaller ball called the jack wins the game). He took off Anne's locket to make the measurement, thus showing Henry that they both fancied her. Henry stumped off crossly.

But Wyatt knew he couldn't win. He wrote a sonnet about it. The first line means, roughly speaking, "Don't tango with me, baby, I belong to the boss".

"Noli me tangere; for Caesar's I am,
And wild for to hold, though I seem tame."

Witty, arrogant, quarrelsome and vain, Henry Howard was a typical Tudor and top poet. He formed a gang of young bloods with Thomas Wyatt's son and others. Their idea of fun was wander round at night smashing windows and attacking people. Henry Howard's close friend was Henry Fitzroy, Henry VIII's bastard son, who was another young raver.

Howard could turn out a slick sonnet as well as being a tough soldier. He fought for the Holy Roman Emperor in Holland in 1544-5 but a lot of his men were killed. He was always getting into trouble and was slung in prison several times for misconduct. He lost his head on a charge of treason in 1547.

Painting was not top priority for Tudors at the start of Henry's reign. So when a young German artist from Augsburg, called Hans Holbein, came over to try his luck, he had trouble finding work.

Things picked up on his second visit in 1532 and he stayed on to become top Tudor painter of the century.

Holbein painted most of Henry's wives, including the picture of Anne of Cleves which fooled Henry into fancying her.

He died of the plague.

NO. 9 – TORRIGIANO

This one-time soldier and genius Italian sculptor came to England to carve Henry VII's tomb. You can still see it in Westminster Abbey.

Torrigiano was a violent hot-head who once punched the great sculptor Michelangelo on the nose, permanently disfiguring him. "I felt the bone and cartilage go down like biscuit under my knuckles," he boasted.

Torrigiano tried to get another great sculptor Cellini to come to England, but Cellini did not want spend time among "such beasts as the English". Torrigiano later went to Spain where he committed suicide rather than fall into the hands of the Inquisition, the cruel Catholic courts set up by the King of Spain.

No. 10 – JOHN SKELTON

John Skelton was not only tutor to the young Henry VIII but a great writer of rumbustious rhymes. He was a clergyman who loved to take the mickey out of people he thought were bad – the greedy, the dishonest and the gluttonous. When he left the court he went to live quietly in Norfolk.

GOODBYE HAL

A HEADY EXPERIENCE

By 1547, Henry was a huge rotting hulk rather like his ship Mary Rose which had recently sunk. He had to be carried everywhere in a litter and hoisted up and down stairs with a winch and a pulley. But despite his hurting leg and his puffy face, he was determined to make sure that his Protestant son Edward became king peacefully at his father's death.

Meanwhile, the money troubles continued. Fighting with the French and Scots cost a fortune and Henry had to sell more and more monasteries. Lots more cash had to be spent on castles to defend the south coast. It was nothing but problems, problems, problems and he was feeling worse everyday.

His personality had got worse as he got older. It was said that he never spared a man his anger or a woman his lust. He could be very nasty. Catherine Parr was once rash enough to defend some Protestant idea in an argument with Henry in his old age. Henry got so angry that he left the room and then gave orders for Catherine to be arrested and sent to the Tower. Luckily, she was tipped off and managed to find Henry and get his forgiveness before anyone got round to carrying out his orders.

When news of Catherine of Aragon's death came through, Henry and Anne Boleyn dressed up in yellow and threw a long party for several days.

A few people managed to like him. Sir Thomas More said, "The King has a way of making every man feel that he is enjoying his special favour."

ROUGH MEDICINE

Henry's health was so bad by 1547 that there was no chance of his doctors saving him. Even if he had lived a much healthier life, they would not have known what to do. Tudor medicine was dodgy...

Most people relied on the herbal knowledge of a wise woman in the village. Other cures included blood-letting, leeches, voiding the stomach, and a good beating.

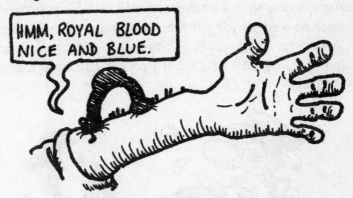

There were two kinds of official doctor in those times, physicians and barber-surgeons. Physicians knew a lot of ancient theory and would recommend cures like virtuous living and a good diet. Barber-surgeons cut hair and did operations. They pulled out teeth with tongs; straightened bone breaks with their hands; chopped off legs and arms. All without anaesthetic, apart from a swig of alcohol.

Wounds were treated by the time-honoured method of cauterization. The barbarous barber-surgeon simply slapped boiling oil or a burning iron to the wounds. After 1536, the French surgeon Ambroise Paré, noticed that soldiers whose wounds were washed and bandaged recovered more quickly than those who had been cauterized. It took fifty years for the sizzling cauterization process to fizzle out in England.

People began to worry that the barber-surgeons were passing on deadly diseases like the plague and syphilis to their hair-cutting clients. A law was passed saying that from now on a barber was a barber and a surgeon a surgeon.

HENRY'S DEATH-BED

Henry was suffering from kidney trouble, gout and circulation problems. "Long since grown corpulent, he was become a burden to himself, and of late lame by reason of a violent ulcer in his leg" said a bystander.

It was against the law to predict the King's death in case this encouraged plots and rebellions. This was awkward now that Henry was actually dying because no-one felt brave enough to tell him so. Eventually, Sir Anthony Denny plucked up the courage. Who would Henry see for his last hours? His wife, Catherine Parr, or his son and heir, Edward VI?

Henry asked for Thomas Cranmer, his faithful archbishop, who came to sit at his bedside. He could no longer speak. Henry died shortly after. From that day on, Cranmer always wore a long white beard as a mark of mourning.

COURT REPORT

Name Henry VIII **Reign** 1509 - 1547

State of country	Could be worse. Religion changed from Catholic to Protestant. Life alright except for vagabonds. OK.
Money matters	Money wasted on silly wars. Poor.
Personal behaviour	Absolutely shocking. Very bad indeed.
Family matters	Henry shows no aptitude for family life. V. poor.
Foreign policy	Broke with Rome. Bashed French and Scots.
Marriages	Six — and only one male heir, Edward VI. V. Poor.
General	Henry has been quite successful in running the country but at a high cost in human lifes. FF. **Headmaster**

102

AFTER HENRY

EDWARD VI THE BOY-KING

Fact No 1: horrible Henry was dead as a very large dodo.

Fact No 2: young King Edward VI crowned in 1547 was only nine years old.

Result: trouble

On Henry's death, power fell into the hands of the King's uncle, Edward Seymour, known as the Duke of Somerset and the Lord Protector.

Somerset and Cranmer wasted no time in rushing lots of Protestant wording into the church service. They got rid of the Mass, and wrote the new services in the Book of Common Prayer. Revolts broke out all over the place, partly against the Protestants' church services and partly against the new government. The rebels were beaten, but it was felt that Somerset hadn't been tough enough. Somerset lost power and was later hanged.

Check out these extra extracts from my Tudor scrap-book.

England smashed in Pinkie push-over   1547

The English army under Lord Protector Somerset has been defeated by the Scots at the battle of Pinkie. The English had invaded Scotland to claim child-bride Mary Queen of Scots for England's youthful monarch Edward VI.

TUDOR TIMES

Sister pleads Pope exemption   1537

Princess Mary, elder sister of boy-King Edward is understood to have written asking to be allowed to continue saying the Roman Catholic mass in private.

Kett rebels camp at Norwich   1549

Protesting against new hedge barriers in Norfolk, a band of desperate farmers has advanced on Norwich. Other rebels have joined them from Suffolk ringing bells and causing trouble on the way.

King in tuberculosis scare   1552

It is reported that twelve-year-old boy-King Edward VI is seriously ill with tuberculosis.

TUDOR TIMES

Protector pushes for power
1537

Edward Seymour, uncle of Edward VI, has been named Duke of Somerset and Lord protector of boy-King Edward, in Seymour family bid for power.

Peasant protestors pasted
1549

Peasant revolts against changes in the Prayer Book and enclosures of land have been smashed by Lord Protector Somerset in lightning northern raid.

Lord Somerset out
1549

Lord Protector Somerset has been eased from office by dashing John, Dudley, Duke of, Northumberland, following landowner outcry over recent peasant revolts. Somerset has shown too much sympathy for the peasants' cause.

Somerset head removed
1552

The late Lord Protector the Duke of Somerset has been hung for treason on charges drawn up by John Dudley Duke of Northumberland.

TUDOR SWOT

Edward was dead clever. An Italian fortune teller described an interview with the young king:

> He could speak many languages when only a child. Along with English, his native tongue, he knew both Latin and French, and he knew some Greek, Italian and Spanish.

Discipline for the boy-king was a slight problem. In Tudor times, teachers loved to flog their pupils. As you couldn't flog a king, even if he was only nine, they came up with the idea of a whipping-boy. This meant choosing a boy the king liked, in this case Barnaby Fitzpatrick, and beating him every time the king misbehaved.

Edward's health was dreadful. He caught tuberculosis. By the end of April, he was spitting blood. From the 11th of June, he ate nothing; by the 14th he was thought to be gone. Oozy sores came out all over his skin, his hair fell off, and then his nails, and afterwards the joints of his toes and fingers. Edward died on 6th July 1553. He was just sixteen years old.

COURT REPORT

Name Edward VI **Reign** 1547 - 1553	
State of country	Troubled. Several uprisings. A difficult job. ok.
Personality	Edward is clever, cool under pressure and ambitious. Impressive.
Foreign policy	Scots behaving. Not all that imaginative. Average.
Marriages	Not applicable ~ too young.
Splendour	As a protestant Edward tended to dress in black. Dull.
Health	Poor. Edward has never a healthy boy.
General	Edward has done very well for his age. Impressive. ΞΨ Headmaster

LADY JANE GREY, NINE DAY WONDER

Lady Jane's problem was that she had Tudor blood. She was a grand-daughter of Henry VIII's sister Mary. In a half baked-plan to keep the crown on a Protestant head following Edward's death, the Duke of Northumberland dragged lovely demure Lady Jane into a forced marriage to his son, Guildford. Innocent Jane was named as Edward's heir in his will and Jane found herself the most reluctant queen in Christendom. Her reign lasted just nine days and then Mary swept to power.

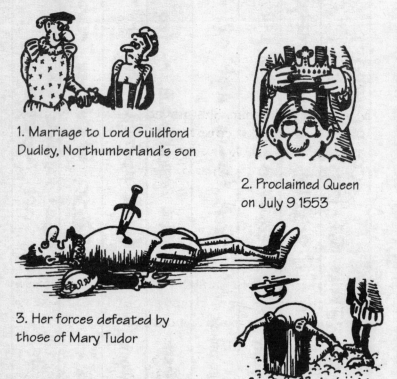

1. Marriage to Lord Guildford Dudley, Northumberland's son

2. Proclaimed Queen on July 9 1553

3. Her forces defeated by those of Mary Tudor

4. Executed, 1554, aged sixteen

BLOODY MARY

THE STINK OF BURNING MARTYRS

The situation so far:

Henry VII   dead
Henry VIII   dead
Edward VI   dead
Mary   in power and ready to go
Elizabeth   still alive and keeping out of trouble

Mary was a Catholic. She moved swiftly to Norfolk where she could count on Catholic support. Meanwhile the whole country rose up in arms. Better a Catholic Tudor daughter of Henry VIII than young Lady Jane Grey, only sixteen and under Northumberland's power.

Mary then swept south at the head of her supporters. She arrived in London to cheers and rejoicing. Poor Mary, it was the best moment of her reign. Within a short time there were already four heads lost to Mary's appetite for executing opponents:

Northumberland
Lady Jane Grey
Lord Guildford Dudley
Thomas Wyatt

MARRIAGE

Mary married Philip II of Spain.

Things wrong with Philip II of Spain:

He was a Catholic
He wasn't very sexy either
He wasn't very fond of Mary

Philip wasn't any old Roman Catholic. He was the most powerful Catholic in the world. The English saw trouble brewing – with good reason. Philip came to England with a hundred and sixty of his own ships and he flew the Spanish flag. The English admiral, Sir William Howard went to meet him with twenty-eight ships. When Howard saw the Spaniards flying their flags in the English Channel, he fired a shot, much to the astonishment of the solemn Spanish king. Howard refused to let them pass until they had taken the flags down.

WE ONLY CAME FOR THE WEDDING!

BOOM!

So England was a Catholic country again. Protestants got ready for persecution. They didn't have long to wait. Nearly three hundred Protestant martyrs were burned during the last four years of Mary's reign.

MARY AND THE MARTYRS

TOLERANCE TABLE

So how bloody was Mary? Did she really make more martyrs than the other Tudor monarchs? Martyrs were people put to death for refusing to believe what they were told to believe by governments. Tudors didn't believe in too much free-thinking. Here is a league table of martyrdoms for heresy, with yearly averages.

TABLE OF MARTYRDOMS			
RULER	MARTYRS	YEARS OF REIGN	AVERAGE MARTYRS PER YEAR
HENRY VII	24	24	1
HENRY VIII	81	38	2.13
EDWARD VI	2	6	0.33
MARY	280	5	56
ELIZABETH	4	44	0.09

If someone expresses a view which contradicts established doctrine in religious matters this is called heresy.

BISHOP BONNER - PROTESTANT FLOGGER

Bishop Bonner was a Protestant-hating churchman who was dragged from prison-retirement by Catholic Mary. He had supported Henry VIII but he still hated Protestants.

As Bishop of London, Bonner got busy putting Protestants to death and cracked coarse jokes as he did it. When Elizabeth eventually became Queen she would not even let him kiss her hand.

Bonner had spent time in prison under Edward VI. The Protestants called him 'Bloody Bonner' while Londoners used the word 'Bonner' for any fat man they saw in the street.

A picture of fat Bonner flogging a protestant appeared in Foxe's 'Book of Martyrs'. Bonner thought it well drawn and said of the artist "A vengeance on the fool, how could he have got my picture drawn so right?"

THAT BURNING FEELING

How did it feel to be martyred?

After your goodbye-speech you
mounted the bonfire, having chosen
whether to wear your outer
garments or just your underwear.

Sometimes you were allowed
to have some gunpowder
hung around your neck to
speed things up.

Alternatively,
some victims were
hoisted up by
pitchforks to spin
out the burning.

QUICK AND SLOW

When two Protestant bishops, Latimer and Ridley, were burned in Oxford, Latimer burned quickly but Ridley slowly. Ridley's brother-in-law put on more wood, but this only damped the fire down. A slow death was thought to be a punishment of God. Latimer said to Ridley before he died:

> Be of good comfort Master Ridley, and play the man. We shall this day light such a candle, by God's grace, in England, as I trust shall never be put out.

THE DEATH OF THOMAS CRANMER

Under Queen Mary, great pressure was put on Thomas Cranmer to accept the Roman Catholic doctrine. Hoping that it would save his life, he signed a paper denying his beliefs.

The authorities decided that Cranmer should be burned to death anyway. The whole break from Rome had been largely his idea. Cranmer then denied his 'denial'. He was taken to a bonfire in Oxford and chained to a stake.

> And when the wood was kindled, and the fire began to burn near him, stretching out his arm he put his right hand into the flame, which he held so steadfast and immovable (saving that once with the same hand he covered his face) that all men might see his hand burned before his body was touched.

Cranmer stood a long time like this, repeating the words, "My unworthy right hand!", until he died.

THE DEATH OF MARY

Mary found it hard to produce a baby. She only managed an imaginary pregnancy, which was sad and pathetic. Philip II didn't spend much time with her. He even flirted with Elizabeth because he knew she might be the next Queen. Mary went to war with France, who then captured Calais, which had been English for two hundred years.

The loss of Calais to the French in Mary's reign seemed like a disaster to the English. Mary was genuinely upset: "When I am dead and opened, you shall find Calais written on my heart." There wasn't long to go. Mary died a tired, old, disappointed woman, in 1558.

By the end, Mary knew that her sister Elizabeth, who acted like a good Catholic during Mary's reign, would turn the country Protestant again after her death. All those Protestant martyrs had been burned for nothing.

COURT REPORT

Name Mary Reign 1516–58

State of country	Weak and divided. Persecution of Protestants deeply resented—	v. poor.
Money matters	Average	
Personal behaviour	Too emotional. Mary is given to seeing things in black and white. Cannot compromise	Poor.
Family matters	No children. False pregnancy raised hopes briefly.	Poor.
Foreign policy	Disastrous. Lost Calais to France	V. Poor.
Marriages	Just one unhappy marriage	Poor
General	Mary has failed to make a good impression and has not shown leadership qualities Headmaster	

A NEW START

ELIZABETH AND GLORY

Queen Elizabeth I came to throne in 1558. She had flaming red hair, she was brilliantly clever – and anything could happen: after all, her mother was Anne Boleyn. What should you expect from a woman whose mother was beheaded by her father?

Elizabeth was the last of the Tudors and a Protestant. She took England into peaceful and prosperous times, which were far more tolerant than those of her father, brother and sister. Her reign was to be a Golden Age – but that's another story.

SO WHY HAD THE COUNTRY GONE PROTESTANT?

Perhaps the main reason was printing. When William Caxton set up the first printing works in London back in 1476, the Catholic leaders were already worried. As Cardinal Wolsey wrote to the Pope:

> The new invention of printing has produced various effects. Men begin to call in question the present faith and tenets of the Church

Which translated means: reading in English helped people to think for themselves. Here's how it went:

1525 Tyndale publishes his New Testament in English.
1535 Coverdale expands this to produce a complete Bible in English.
1537 A Bible is licensed by Henry VIII for general reading by the English people.
1539 The Great Bible, produced by Coverdale goes into every Church.
1558 Protestant Elizabeth mounts the throne.

The Bishop of Durham tried to put a stop to it by sending his agent to Antwerp to buy up all the copies of Tyndale's Bible he could find. He bought all Tyndale's unsold copies, in order to destroy them. This gave Tyndale the money to produce a new edition with better illustrations!

TUDORS – THE SCORE SO FAR (BY 1558)

STATE OF THE NATION
Powerful. No civil wars. No major rebellions.

STATE OF THE CROWN
Tudors accepted as rightful kings and queens.

STATE OF RELIGION
Protestant revolution accomplished.

STATE OF THE PEOPLE
Not very free.

VERDICT
On the whole and so far, Tudors were a good thing.
England was now a strong independent country and
ready for greater things.

Over to you Elizabeth!

NEXT TIME, READ ALL ABOUT ME AND MY REIGN, FOLKS!

STATE THE DATE

THE EARLY YEARS

1485	Henry VII wins Battle of Bosworth.
1509	Death of Henry VII. Henry VIII becomes King. Marries Catherine of Aragon (Cath). 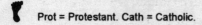
1512	Butcher's boy Wolsey (Cath) becomes chief minister.
1513	War with France and Scotland.
1516	Birth of Henry VIII's daughter Mary (Cath).
1520	Field of the Cloth of Gold. Showing off.

THE BREAK WITH ROME

1525	Anne Boleyn (Prot) appears at court. Trouble !
1529	Fall and death of Wolsey (Cath).
1533	Henry VIII marries Anne Boleyn (Prot) and rejects the Pope (Cath, of course). Daughter Elizabeth (Prot) is born. Thomas Cromwell (Prot) chief minister.
1535	Execution of Sir Thomas More (Cath) and others.
1536	Execution of Anne Boleyn (Prot). Marriage to Jane Seymour (Prot).
1536-39	Dissolution of the monasteries.
1537	Birth of Edward VI (Prot) and death of Jane Seymour. English Bible (Prot) published.

Prot = Protestant. Cath = Catholic.

THE CATHOLIC RECOVERY

1540   Marriage and divorce with Anne of Cleves (Prot). Thomas Cromwell (Prot) executed. Marriage to Catherine Howard (Cath).

1541   Execution of Catherine Howard's lovers.

1542   Execution of Catherine Howard (Cath).

1543   Renewed persecution of Protestants. Marriage to Catherine Parr (devout but moderate).

1544   War with France and Scotland.

EDWARD VI AND THE PROT PROTECTORS

1546   Suppression of Catholics on King's Council.

1547   Death of Henry VIII. Accession of Edward VI (Prot) with Duke of Somerset (Prot) as Lord Protector.

1549   First Book of Common Prayer (Prot) published. Duke of Northumberland (Prot) replaces Somerset.

1552   Somerset (Prot) executed. The Second Book of Common Prayer.

1553   Death of Edward VI (Prot). Jane Grey (Prot) is proclaimed and defeated.

THE REIGN OF BLOODY MARY

1553   Mary Tudor (Cath) becomes Queen. Catholic Mass restored.

1554   Sir Thomas Wyatt (Prot) leads rebellion. Jane Grey executed (Prot). Elizabeth (Prot) sent to the Tower. Mary marries Philip II of Spain (Cath). Cardinal Pole (Cath) returns from Rome.

1555-8   280 Protestants, including Cranmer, burned.

1558   The French capture Calais. Death of Mary (Cath). Accession of sister Elizabeth (Prot).

GRAND QUIZ

Now that you've finished this book, why not test your Tudor knowledge and find out if you've become a Tudor expert.

1) What is the Tudor Rose?

a) a lovely pink flower with a beautiful scent
b) a ceiling ornament
c) a flower with red and white petals

2) Who was John Skelton?

a) Henry VIII's tutor
b) Henry VIII's whipping boy
c) a very thin court musician

3) Which Tudor ate lots of boiled vegetables?

a) Henry VIII
b) Anne Boleyn
c) Nobody

4) What was a board?

a) a noisy woman
b) a boring man
c) a table-top

5) What were the Tudor rules of football?

a) no less than fifty players on each side
b) there weren't any
c) get the ball back to the other village

6) What was the Mary Rose?

a) a special type of Tudor rose
b) an instrument of torture
c) a ship

7) What was Tudor beer?

a) a new drink flavoured with
   hops
b) an old drink, replaced by ale
c) an expensive drink for noblemen only

8) Why did Henry divorce Catherine of Aragon?

a) because she had too many babies
b) because she was unfaithful
c) because she didn't have a son

9) Who kept toenail clippings?

a) Henry's servants
b) Henry kept Anne Boleyn's
c) a monastery

10) Who touched a Princess with his
    bare foot?

a) the Duc de Longueville
b) Cardinal Wolsey
c) Thomas Cromwell

11) Who liked bathing?

a) Henry VIII
b) Anne Boleyn
c) nobody

12) Who got beheaded?

a) common criminals
b) important people
c) anyone

13) Who hated foreigners?

a) Italians
b) Germans
c) Englishmen

14) Who had to kiss the cat?

a) another cat
b) an Italian
c) a Dutchman called Erasmus

15) What was an interlude?

a) A short stay
b) A pause between the acts of a play
c) A kind of a dance

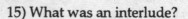

ANSWERS:

Are you a Tudor expert yet?
If you got more than eight questions
right you're well on the way!

1) c, see page 10
2) b, page 14
3) c, page 25
4) c, page 26
5) b, page 33
6) c, page 39
7) a, page 41
8) c, page 43
9) c, page 45
10) a, page 58
11) c, page 60
12) b, page 75/6
13) c, page 80
14) c, page 81
15) c, page 91

INDEX

What they don't tell you about

ELIZABETH I

HER FRIENDS AND RELATIONS

By Bob Fowke

Dedicated to clever girls with
long pointed noses everywhere.

Hodder
Children's
Books

A division of Hodder Headline Limited

Hallo, my name's Harry Hunks. I'm a bear, a famous fighting bear. It's *grrrrrrrrreat* to meet you. I know a lot about the reign of Elizabeth I from all the different kinds of people who came to watch me fight in the bear ring. Elizabeth was no *honey*, but she and her friends were *furociously* fascinating. So come with me and find out more about her. We may only *scratch* the surface of her story, but there's plenty of amazing facts to *bite* into if you read on...

What They Don't Tell You About Elizabeth I first published as a single volume in Great Britain in 1995 by Hodder Children's Books.

CONTENTS

 Whenever you see this sign in the book it means there are some more details at the FOOT of the page, like here.

WATCH OUT FOR THE LANKY LADY!

HOW IT ALL BEGAN

It's two o'clock in the morning one day in 1601, bedtime for most honest citizens. A bony old woman prowls around her private room. Every now and then she pauses, muttering, and stabs a rusty sword deep into the rich wall-hangings. She fears that enemies lurk in the shadows behind, waiting to kill her.

BRIGHT ORANGE WIG

BAD SKIN DUE TO USING TOO MUCH MERCURY AND TURPENTINE MAKE-UP.

BAD TEETH DUE TO THE NEW FASHION OF EATING A LOT OF SUGAR.

The old lady is Elizabeth I, the last of the Tudors and the greatest Queen of England ever.

How did it all begin?...

Buttered baby

It all started one Sunday in September 1533, at Greenwich Palace on the south bank of the river Thames, where Queen Anne Boleyn lay in her royal bed. The midwives, who help at births, had trimmed their nails and smeared pig-fat or butter on their hands to make them slippery, ready to help deliver a new royal baby.

But wait –
Two reasons to be nervous:

1. The father-to-be was King Henry VIII and he wanted a boy to inherit his crown.

2. Henry VIII had a very bad temper.

The new baby arrived at around four in the afternoon. As soon as people heard the news, church bells were pealed and bonfires were lit in celebration of the birth. The crowd went wild, but in all the happy throng two people weren't celebrating; Henry and Anne were fed up – the baby was a little girl.

FAMILY GALLERY

Baby Elizabeth was Henry's second royal child. His eldest was Mary, daughter of Henry's first wife.

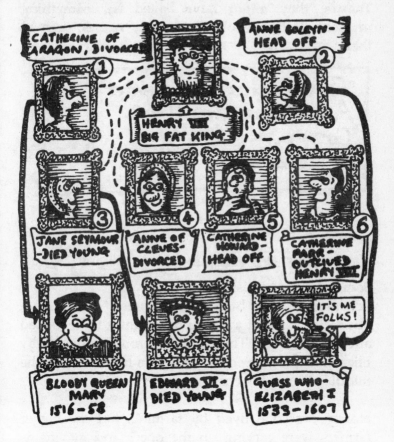

Henry had one other child called Henry Fitzroy by a mistress called Bessie Blount. He died when he was seventeen, poor cub.

NAME GAMES

Elizabeth was christened when she was three days old. Her parents nearly called her Mary although, being Tudors, they might have called her something unusual. Tudor people liked fancy names, such as these:

Temperance Slaughter
Appelina Proudlove
Cognata Stockes
Cassandra Potter

VAGAMONKS AND VAGABONDS

Soon after the baptism, because her mother was busy being Queen of England, Elizabeth was sent away to the country to be looked after by an aunt. The country through which baby Elizabeth was carried to her aunt's house was in the middle of some big changes.

Nearly everyone lived by farming, but the bigger farmers were carving up the open land into fields surrounded by hedges or walls. The area of common land left over for poor men to farm was shrinking. Hordes of landless men were forced to wander the countryside as vagabonds. On top of that, Henry had recently decided to shut all the monasteries and take their riches. So unemployed monks joined the hordes of vagabonds.

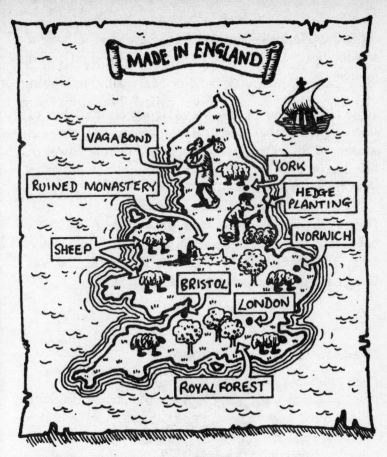

Map labels: MADE IN ENGLAND, VAGABOND, YORK, RUINED MONASTERY, HEDGE PLANTING, NORWICH, SHEEP, BRISTOL, LONDON, ROYAL FOREST

A CHOP OFF THE OLD BLOCK

QUESTION:

What do you do if your name is Henry VIII and your wife doesn't give birth to a son?

ANSWER:

Chop her head off.

When Elizabeth was one-year-old, her mother Anne nearly had a baby boy, but this little nearly-brother died before he was born. From then on Henry gave up on Anne. He looked round for a new wife to have a son for him, and he soon found a girl he liked called Jane Seymour.

To get Anne out of the way, Henry accused her of sleeping with other men and after a short trial she was sentenced to death. She was beheaded at the Tower of London on 19th May 1536. They brought a swordsman over from France specially.

Henry divorced Anne two days before she was beheaded. So now Elizabeth as well as her elder sister, Mary, had lost her right to inherit the throne. She was two years and eight months old.

KID'S
STUFF

Elizabeth had plenty of time for her education. It was quite common for young royals to learn more than one language, but Elizabeth was extra brainy. She learned to speak lots of them.

GREEK- QUITE WELL

ENGLISH
(OF COURSE)

SPANISH-
A LITTLE

FRENCH- FLUENTLY

WELSH – NOT
MUCH

ITALIAN- FLUENTLY

FLEMISH-
NOT MUCH

LATIN-
FLUENTLY

GIRLS' SKOOL

During Elizabeth's childhood most middle and upper class girls learned to read and write. This was because

there were lots of books around due to the invention of printing. Books on subjects like cookery, household management and needlework started to be written specially for women.

Girls' education could be tough. Many teachers believed that it was important to beat girls as well as boys – especially girls, according to the tutor of Elizabeth's older sister, Mary. (Elizabeth was luckier; her tutor didn't believe in that sort of thing).

Most working-class girls never got the chance to learn to read and write at all, but even rich girls didn't have to learn quite as much as Elizabeth. I picked up this timetable which some young aristocrat dropped into the bear-pit...

APPELINA'S TIMETABLE

7.00 AM
French master
arrives

9.00 AM
Dancing
master

10.00 AM
Lessons on
the virginals

LUNCH!

4.00 PM
Lute and viol de
gamba lesson

SUPPER!

9.00 PM
Bedtime

13

As well as languages and subjects like dancing and music, Elizabeth had to learn maths, history, geography, architecture and astronomy. She ended up knowing a lot more than most upper-class boys.

Boys' skool
Two questions...

1. Do you hate school?

2. Are you a boy?

If the answer to both questions is yes – count your blessings, brother. You would have hated school a lot more if you had been a Tudor. Girls were taught at home, but boys' schools were really tough. School started as early as five or six in the morning and went on till five or six at night, with two hours for lunch.

The Tudor Class-room
Flogging and other physical punishments were a normal part of school life. These are some typical Tudor punishments:

1. being pulled by the hair ▼

2. being lashed over the face ◄

3. being beaten about the head with a great rod ◄

4. being struck on the lips with a ruler. ▼

Animals were punished too. People thought that, just like children, it was good for their characters. For instance a dog which killed a lamb might be locked up with a fierce ram to teach it better manners.

DON'T SPEAK TILL YOU'RE SPOKEN TO!

Being a royal, Elizabeth had her own household, even though she was young. She was treated with respect by the people who looked after her. She was lucky; in all non-royal houses young people had to be very careful how they behaved.

Amaze your parents. Try out this Tudor guide to good behaviour...

> ### TUDOR KIDS
>
> *Stand up in the presence of your parents.*
>
> *Call your parents Sir and Madame.*
>
> *Eat at a separate table.*
>
> *Serve your parents at table, if there are no servants to do it.*

YOUR SERVANT, SIR

A lot of servants were needed to run big houses. Most of them were young people who were not always much older than the children of the house. The master and mistress were responsible for their young servants, as they were for their own children. Nearly three quarters of all boys and more than half of all girls between the ages of twenty and twenty-four were servants. There were more boys than girls because boys were useful for defence, as armed retainers. Most country villages only had a handful of young men living in them. The rest were away working as servants in towns or big houses.

Even the rich sent their children to serve in other people's houses as pages or sometimes as ladies in waiting. Servants and their masters lived closely together. In fact stewards and other top servants were more like courtiers or friends. Elizabeth always had a number of people like this living with her. Her ladies-in-waiting were always noble women.

SERVANT RULES

There were still rules to be followed. For example:

1. People 'gave the wall' to their superiors if they met them in the street. This meant letting them have the side of the pavement furthest away from passing horses and carts.

2. Servants called their master and mistress by their full name and title .

3. Masters and Mistresses called their servants by their first names.

4. Servants could be fined if they did wrong:

One penny	swearing, untidy dress, leaving a bed unmade after 8.00am
Two pennies	not going to family prayers
Six pennies	being late to serve dinner

The terms 'Mr' and 'Mrs' are shortened forms of Master and Mistress.

If you couldn't play with other children, there were always animals to play with. Tudor houses were full of them and Tudor kids had time to play even though their hours of work were long.

CAT FANATICS AND DOG SNOBS

Hounds and spaniels were the top dogs. There were clear class distinctions. For instance, in 1567 the Mayor of Liverpool ordered that all mastiffs (a large fierce dog) and watchdogs had to be tied up so that they didn't hurt any posh hounds.

Tabbies were the top cats because only the rich could afford them. The first tabbies had only recently been brought to England from the East. Whatever their class, pets were often very well treated. One merchant in Leeds had holes cut through all the doors in his house so that his cats could wander freely.

WARNING TO TUDOR CATS

Not everyone liked cats. One school book had this simple sentence in Latin for translation: 'I hate cats'.

TEEN SCENES

WOULD YOU LIKE TO BE YOUR FATHER'S WIDOW'S WIDOWER'S WIFE?

Henry VIII died in 1547. He was succeeded by his son, Edward, Elizabeth's younger brother. Being a girl, Elizabeth never expected to become Queen.

While all this was happening Elizabeth was looked after by Henry's widow, Catherine Parr, who remarried, this time to handsome, red-bearded Lord Thomas Seymour. Teenage Elizabeth had a crush on teasing Lord Thomas. He used to make her laugh; once he and Catherine chased her round the garden then cut her gown into little pieces.

Catherine died in childbirth in 1548, and soon afterwards Thomas asked Elizabeth to marry him. As Elizabeth's husband he would have a chance of becoming King if young King Edward died. She put him off saying she was not ready. Desperate for power, Thomas then plotted to kidnap Edward.

Thomas' plots were discovered. He was beheaded on 20th March 1549.

19

SPOT THE DIFFERENCE!

CATHOLIC MARY

Young King Edward VI didn't last long. He died on 6th July 1553 of a disease called tuberculosis. Within days Elizabeth's elder sister, Mary, was made Queen. Mary was a staunch Roman Catholic.

PROTESTANT ELIZABETH

Elizabeth was a Protestant. Once Mary came to the throne, Elizabeth was in danger. Mary was determined to stamp out all traces of Protestantism in England and started on a programme of burning Protestants.

SQUASH THE PROTS!

In 1553, when Edward died and Mary came to the throne, Europe was about to be torn apart in a deadly war between Catholics and Protestants.

Catholics hated Protestants because Protestants had turned their backs on the Roman Catholic church. They burned and tortured them to try to turn them into Catholics. Protestants hated Catholics because they thought that the Roman Catholic religion was corrupt. Protestants burned and tortured too, although not so much.

To make matters worse there was a new hard-line breed of Protestant. These were the Puritans. They wore dark clothes, went to church a lot and disapproved of people having fun. Elizabeth was never a Puritan even though she was a Protestant.

A party of prim Puritans

Some visitors to my show dropped these newspaper cuttings. I picked them up so you could have a look...

The Elizabethan Echo

DUTCH IN FREEDOM FIGHT– 1568

The Netherlands was part of the Spanish Empire. Most Dutch people were Protestants and their Spanish rulers tried to burn them back into the Catholic Church. In 1568 the Dutch started the revolt which would lead to Holland becoming an independent country.

HUGUENOTS HAMMERED 1562-98

French Protestants were called Huguenots. There were lots of them in France. They were unpopular, and the French government tried to crush them. The Wars of Religion went on for thirty-six years and forced many of the best French Protestants to leave the country.

PARIS PROTS MASSACRED – 1572

On 24th August, Saint Bartholomew's Day, 3000 Huguenots were massacred in cold blood in Paris, and many more in the French provinces. This event sent shock-waves through England.

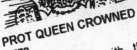

PROT QUEEN CROWNED 1558

Henry VIII split with the Pope, but he was never a true Protestant. Edward had been a Protestant king, but too young to rule. It was only after Elizabeth came to power that England became the most powerful of all the Protestant countries.

MEANWHILE...TO THE TOWER!

Queen Mary's health was bad and if Mary died, Elizabeth would become the next Queen of England. Elizabeth was accused of plotting against her sister and sent to the Tower of London. For two months she was shut up and in daily fear of being beheaded. Her prison cell was a gloomy room opposite a passageway leading to three toilets which hung high over the walls of the moat.

Desperately Elizabeth pleaded for her life, and at last she was allowed to leave the Tower. It had been a narrow escape.

While Mary's health got worse, Elizabeth was shut up in a house in the country . At last, one morning in 1558, a messenger galloped from London to where she was staying. He carried Mary's engagement ring – proof that Mary had died of cancer.

GREAT, SHE'S SNUFFED IT!

Very important nobles whose presence was inconvenient were quite often kept under 'house arrest' like this, rather than being imprisoned like a criminal.

24

HOME
COMFORTS

A MAGIC MOMENT

Elizabeth believed in astrology  . She asked the famous scientist Dr John Dee to tell her the best day for her coronation. Although Dr Dee was a scientist, he liked to dabble in magic and astrology as well. He had a crazy friend called Kelly who wore a black cap to hide the fact that his ears had been cut off  . Egged on by Kelly, Dr Dee would try to read messages from spirits in a crystal ball. He chose Sunday 15th January for the coronation.

So on Sunday 15th January 1559 the crown of England was placed on Elizabeth's head in Westminster Abbey. Outside the crowd went wild; people were delighted to have a Protestant queen after bloody, Catholic Queen Mary. Bells peeled and brightly coloured hangings fluttered from every

---

 Astrologists believe that the position of the stars in the sky affects how things happen on Earth.

 Cutting off bits of the body was a common punishment for theft.

window in London. People fought to cut out bits from a posh blue carpet which had been laid for Elizabeth to walk over from Westminster Hall to Westminster Abbey. The Duchess of Norfolk, who was holding up Elizabeth's cloak, kept tripping over the holes in the carpet.

PALACES THAT PONG

Now that she was Queen, Elizabeth took possession of at least six palaces:

Richmond; good for hunting ▶

▲ *Whitehall with its grounds, the largest palace in Europe*

▲ *Greenwich by the river Thames*

◀ *Hampton Court, stolen by old king Henry*

▲ *Nonsuch built by old king Henry*

There were about 1,500 people in the royal household, so the palaces got very crowded. The floors of the great halls were covered in rushes, and the rushes became disgustingly sticky with bits of food and dog mess. Things soon got very smelly. After about six weeks it was time to move on. Then all the mess could be shovelled out and the palace generally cleaned and 'sweetened'.

The royal court travelled from one palace to another with side-journeys to visit the houses of rich nobles further away. When on the move, the court travelled about twelve miles a day. All the furniture came too;

If Elizabeth came to visit and your house wasn't big enough, some of the courtiers and servants camped in the grounds or lodged in nearby villages and towns. It could cost you a pot of money.

four hundred wagons and 2,400 pack horses were needed to carry everything.

A ROOM AT THE TOP

In Elizabeth's time things were getting more comfortable than they had been in the past, especially at court and in the houses of the rich. Piped water was installed at Richmond Palace, and at Hardwick House a horse-wheel powered pump fed water to a special room beside a new hall.

But Richmond Palace and Hardwick House were a bit unusual. Life in the houses of most noblemen improved more slowly; at least in the great halls the rushes were now changed once a month, instead of new rushes just being layed on top of the old, as in the Middle Ages. There's a description of a hall eighty years later – things are still very basic: marrow bones, scraps of food and dog mess are still trodden into the rushes, there are litters of kittens on the chairs, hawks' hoods, bells and hats full of pheasants eggs on the tables, and the whole place is swarming with hawks, hounds, spaniels and terriers.

Many cottages had a single downstairs room. The furniture of a poor family might be just a few stools, a trestle table, a straw mattress, a fire with an iron cooking pot and a beaten earth floor. There would probably be a few chickens scratching about and possibly the odd cat or dog.

"THINGS I WANT – SOME COMFY NEW THINGS"
BY A TUDOR

IMPORTED PILE CARPETS

CUPS MADE OF PEWTER INSTEAD OF WOOD.

FEATHER BEDS INSTEAD OF STRAW PALLETS.

CHIMNEYS

These were still very rare and definitely a luxury.

LIFE AT THE BOTTOM

In 1597 one of the first flush toilets in the world was installed in Richmond Palace for Elizabeth's personal use. It was designed by her godson, Sir John Harington.

For a long time not many people followed her example, and there was still a lot of 'pissing in chimneys'. The rich might have a cupboard or stool-house next to their bedroom with a chamber pot inside which had to be emptied frequently.

But most people used earth toilets, where a bucket full of earth or cinders was thrown down the hole after use

to cover up the waste ◄. Many earth toilets had more than one hole to make best use of the space beneath. Every few weeks or months a 'nightsoil' man would come and

 Some toilets never got cleaned out properly; modern specialist historians investigate the dried out waste beneath old toilets, looking for things which may have been dropped in by accident.

30

dig out the waste and remove it on a cart.

There were no proper sewage pipes to carry away liquid sewage, which might leak anywhere. Drinking water from wells was often polluted, and so much muck flowed into the river Thames that clothes washed in it smelled of sewage afterwards.

Some waste products had their uses however. Toilets often had a small extra hole with a pan underneath to collect the urine. The urine was used to make lye,

which was used for washing clothes. It was specially good for getting rid of greasy stains. Other things used to make lye included pigeon or hen dung, bran and wood-ash. Apple-wood ash gave the whitest wash.

Clothes were folded into a wooden tub. The lye was poured over the clothes, squidged around a bit, then drawn off at the bottom through a tap. This process was repeated until the lye came through clean.

LEISURE

PLEASURES

HAVING FUN, THE TUDOR WAY!

– BUT FIRST, A TIME TO DINE

Elizabeth hated getting up early. She liked to laze in bed till late in the morning, then she nibbled a breakfast of white bread and butter with a meat soup and either wine or beer. Nothing made her more grumpy than to give her strong beer; she had weak beer specially brewed.

Dinner was the meal that mattered. It started at midday or even earlier. Among the upper classes it could go on for three hours. The laying of the royal dinner table was a major procedure. Special officials spread the cloth, carried the bread and other tasks. They bowed and knelt as if the queen were present,

and there was more bowing when she arrived. She removed all her rings and washed her hands in a gold basin before she ate.

The food, when it came, was often cold. Kitchens tended to be in separate buildings because of the danger of fire. At Windsor, meals were sometimes cooked in a public oven in town, more than ten minutes walk away.

POISON! BEWARE!

Dishes were brought to the royal table by servants called the *yeomen of the guard*. As they entered the room, a lady with a tasting-fork made each yeoman eat a piece of the food he was carrying to test it for poison.

MEAT WITH YOUR MEAT

Elizabethans ate mountains of meat if they could afford it. As well as all the animals people eat today, they ate hedgehogs, heron, peacocks and song birds. In fact they ate pretty well anything with legs or wings except insects. Different types of meat were thought to have different effects on the eater; beef was good for Englishmen because it was thought to be lusty and lively, but hare was meant to make you feel depressed.

Meat was boiled, roasted, baked in pies and made into jelly, which was very popular. Roast meat was turned on a spit before the fire. Often dogs turned the spits by running in dog wheels. Hot coals were sometimes put beneath their paws to make them run faster.

By old church tradition, Fridays and Saturdays were fish days when it was forbidden to eat meat. In 1560,

BAD MANNERS. HOW TO BE RUDE AT THE COURT OF QUEEN ELIZABETH...

BLOW NOSE ON KNAPKIN

WIPE MOUTH WITH SLEEVE

DRINK TOO MUCH

WOODEN TRENCHER

GREAT SALT

Wednesday became a fish day as well. This was so that fishermen could sell more fish. Fishermen were needed by the government because they could be used as sailors in time of war.

GETTING STUFFED

While the rich were stuffing themselves with meat, wine and beer at three hour lunch breaks, ordinary people were – stuffing themselves as well. Foreigners were amazed at the amount of food English people could cram down their throats, especially Londoners who ate more meat than country people.

And country people, although their diet was more limited than Londoners', still ate better than people on the continent of Europe. Some English peasants ate better than German nobility according to one German

visitor, even though poor cottagers and labourers ate very little meat. The poor lived mainly on bread made from rye or barley flour and 'white meats' which was the term for dairy products with the occasional chicken or piece of bacon.

And what did people drink to slosh it all down? Beer! Everyone drank it, for breakfast, dinner and supper. Even children could drink as much beer as they liked if it was available. Normally people drank from horn beakers or black leather 'jacks'. They drank wine too but it was more expensive.

HOW THE POTATO WAS MISUNDERSTOOD

Most people think it was Elizabeth's favourite Sir Walter Raleigh, who introduced the potato to Britain, but it was in fact his friend, mathematician Thomas Harriot. Thomas had gone to America to help start the colony of Virginia, which was Walter Raleigh's pet project.

One day Elizabeth's chamberlain invited some nobles to try Harriot's new vegetable. However no one knew how to cook it. They used the leaves and stems (which are mildly poisonous) and left the potatoes in the ground. All the guests left with stomach aches. The potato didn't recover its reputation for more than a hundred years.

SWEET TREATS

Elizabeth, like most top Tudors, loved sweets. There was less honey around than there used to be because her father had closed down the monasteries; the monks had needed a lot of bees to make beeswax for monastery candles.

Honey had been the traditional sweetener, so a new source of sweetness was needed. Starting in the 1540s, sugar was produced in London. Coarse imported sugar was purified into large white lumps of up to six kilos each. These were then modelled by skilled cooks into fantastic sugary creations. The cooks could model birds, animals and fruit out of sugar. Even plates, playing cards and wine glasses could be made, using a crisp type of sugar known as sugar plate. They might be decorated with paint, penwork and gilding.

The amount of sugar eaten in England would have been about half a kilo per person per year – if most of it had not been eaten by the likes of Elizabeth, who ate far too much. The result was terrible tooth decay for top people. Elizabeth ended her life with a row of black rotten stumps in her mouth, and so did many others.

RECIPE FOR TOOTHPASTE

Rub ashes of rosemary or powdered alabaster onto your teeth with your finger.

TUDOR TIME-OFF

Elizabethans loved games and holidays, but Puritans, who were extreme Protestants, thought they were all the work of the devil. Elizabeth was no Puritan; she still joined in the festivities on Mayday, even when she was an old lady.

DEVIL'S DIARY

THE WEEK AFTER EASTER
On Hoch Monday, the day after Easter, the men of Reading would grab the women and hold them captive until they paid a ransom. On Hoch Tuesday the women did the same to the men.

MAY 1ST
On Mayday people would bring a tree into their town or village, pulled by oxen. The tree was decorated with flowers and herbs and set upright. There was a wild party which went on all day and night.

NOVEMBER 17TH - JOUST A MINUTE
A public holiday was held each year on the date Elizabeth came to the throne, Accession Day. There was always jousting. Courtiers, mounted on massive horses, rode at each other at full gallop and were given points according to where their lances struck.

DECEMBER 25TH
The festivities at Christmas went on for twelve days. There were no Christmas trees. Instead there was a Yule Log, a massive log big enough to burn for twelve days. The peasants also chose a Lord of Misrule whose job was to make fun of the proper lord and the normal rules of society.

SPORTS FIRSTS

Early versions of many modern sports were played in Elizabethan times:

1. Bowls was the national game and it was played everywhere. Most large houses had a bowling green.

2. Stoolball, probably the ancestor of cricket, was popular in Sussex. (It still is).

3. Skittles was played in pub yards. It is the ancestor of ten-pin bowling.

4. Fives, which is a bit like squash but played with a gloved hand, was very popular.

5. Real tennis came from France. It was originally called *Tenez* which means 'hold on' in French. Real tennis is still played today. It's an indoor game where the ball is bounced off the walls as well as being hit over the net.

Bear-baiting was popular with all classes of people. Elizabeth loved it. She even kept a team of bears to use in her own bear-pit. People would set fierce dogs on us, and we fought them off with our claws. Some of us became famous, like me and my friends Little Bess of Bromley and George Stone.

The Elizabethan Echo

Circulation 2 million

Sports Review

Fierce Football

Football was very popular. Big matches could be terrifying, because there were few rules in early football. In Pembrokeshire they played with a hard wooden ball, boiled in fat to make it slippery. There were as many as a thousand players on each side. They cut their hair and beards short so that the opposing team couldn't get a grip on them. People suffered dreadful injuries in football games.

Bishop in Rabbit Ban Row

Golf was already popular in Scotland. The Archbishop of St Andrews had to limit rabbit warren construction on the St Andrew's Golf Links to allow space for golf, football and archery.

A Hunting We Will Go

Hunting was the sport for top people, including Elizabeth who was mad about it. When young she would gallop with the men. Later she sat and waited for the animal to be driven toward her. She always liked to kill the prey, shooting it with an arrow. Hunting days would often start with a big open air breakfast. The butter would set off early with a massive train of waggons, carts and mules, all loaded with things for a feast.

Special rabbit warrens were often built in Tudor times, because rabbits were a popular sort of meat.

41

TAKE NOTE

Elizabethans loved music and dancing, whether it was mad dancing behind a Lord of Misrule, or stately dancing at court, normally after supper. Dancing was Elizabeth's main form of exercise.

TOP OF THE TUDOR POPS

Thomas Tallis, 1505-85 was the tutor of *William Byrd*. He held an honorary position, 'gentleman of the royal chapel', which gave him time to compose. He wrote mainly church music, but some other tunes as well.

William Byrd, c.1543-1623. Although he was a Catholic, he became organist of Lincoln Cathedral, which was Protestant Church of England like all English cathedrals. Later he became joint organist of the royal chapel with Tallis.

John Dowland, 1563-1626. He played the lute and wrote songs. He also travelled a lot, working for eight years as a lutenist at the Danish court.

At court, if there was no dancing after supper, they might play games such as Hoodman Blind (Blind Man's Buff) or Dun in the Mire, which involved trying to lift a heavy log and drop it on someone's toes.

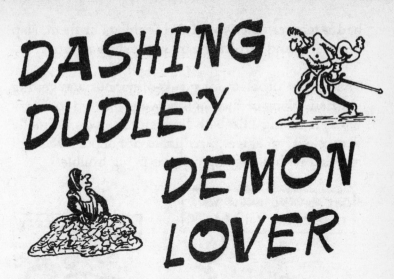

DASHING DUDLEY DEMON LOVER

FANCY CLOTHES AND FREE WOMEN

From day one of her reign Elizabeth made sure she was in control of her court. Everyone had to bow or curtsey and to show proper respect.

She was hardly ever alone. Even at night one of her ladies in waiting would sleep in the room with her, and four chamber maids would be on call. There was always the threat of danger; once a mad sailor holding a dagger burst into her chamber. Fortunately it turned out that he was only mad with love for her.

Elizabeth's closest companions were her maids-of-honour. They were a loud bunch of young noblewomen, who used to fool about in their bedroom at night and annoy the Vice-Chamberlain, Sir William Knollys, who slept in the next-door room. Elizabeth

43

had a temper; she would throw things at them, slap their faces and box their ears when she was cross.

The biggest problem for maids-of-honour was getting married. None of the nobility were allowed to marry without asking Elizabeth first, and she was normally very slow to agree. Any maid-of-honour who got married without asking her was in big trouble.

Elizabeth herself never married. She said she was married to England and she became known as the Virgin Queen – which didn't mean that she didn't like men. Far from it; she wanted all her courtiers to be as handsome and dashing as possible, and the handsomest and dashingest of all was Robert Dudley, known as 'the gypsy' because of his dark skin.

INTERESTED IN GARDENING

TALL

LOVE OF JOUSTING

INTEREST IN ARCHITECTURE

NOBLE BROW

FAIR HAIR

FINE MOUSTACHE

MANLY SHOULDERS

NICE LIPS

VERY LONG LEGS

Elizabeth was mad about Dudley. In 1560 his wife (yes, he was already married) was found dead at the bottom of the staircase of his house in the country. People said he had had her killed so that he would be free to marry Elizabeth, but there's no evidence to prove him guilty.

Later he married again, to a woman called Lettuce (another mad Tudor name) whom Elizabeth always called 'the she-wolf'. But Elizabeth even forgave him for getting married, and Dudley, or the Earl of Leicester as he became, was her favourite and one of the most powerful men in the country until he died.

FASHION PARADE – WOMEN

Elizabeth worked on her image like a modern film star. It helped to keep her in power. Her clothes were a part of that image. When she died there were more than three thousand dresses in her cupboards. In public she wore incredibly expensive gowns and behaved in a stately, goddess-like way. Everyone at court was expected to dress expensively, though her maids-of-honour had to dress in black or white so as to make her stand out. All this was for the public; in private she liked to dress quite simply.

A farthingale was a frame made of wooden or whale-bone hoops used to extend women's skirts.

FASHION PARADE – MEN

Men wore puffy pants and a cod piece  . They nearly always wore a sword and a dagger. Naturally no one was allowed to wear a sword too near the queen. The clothes of both men and women grew flashier and flashier as Elizabeth's reign went on.

The rapier was a type of light sword. It was as well to be prepared, people were always getting killed in sword fights. Some ruffians would carry two swords and two daggers. When men like this had too much to drink, things could get very dangerous. In 1580 a law limited the maximum sword length to three feet (nearly a metre).

 The codpiece was a lump of stuffed material which jutted from the front of men's pants.

Make-up Tips

Court was a paradise for pick-ups. It was full of young people when Elizabeth came to the throne. Everyone flirted and dressed in their best clothes. The fashionable look for women was a white skin, thin eyebrows and red lips. Elizabeth had most of these, but other women had to try harder:

- For whiter skin – a powder of ground pigs' jawbones, asses' milk and beeswax. Or why not try a vicious mixture of white lead and vinegar?

- For fairer hair - bleach hair in the sun, but be sure to keep your nice white face in shadow by using a mask held in place by a button between the teeth.

- For red lips – try red cinnabar ﹡.

- To remove spots and freckles – birch tree sap or sublimate of mercury ﹡ ﹡.

- To smooth skin damaged by long use of the above make-ups – apply a glaze of egg-whites, then draw on thin blue lines to look like veins.

- To make eyes sparkle – use drops of deadly nightshade.

- To make teeth ultra-white – rub with powdered brick coral, or powdered alabaster.

The proper chemical name for this substance is 'crystalline mercuric sulphide'. In colour it is bright scarlet.

This badly damaged the skin.

MARRIED LIFE

Aristocratic women usually married in their late teens. They had to marry who they were told to, although marriages completely against their will were disapproved of.

Marriage itself was not so important as nowadays. It was the engagement which tied the knot. For the ceremony a bride would wear her best dress, with her hair down as a sign that she was a virgin. White weddings started in Tudor times.

Once married, women had to obey their husbands, but they still had a lot of power in the home, looking after the servants, managing the household finances and acting as doctor to family and servants, which might involve setting broken bones and treating wounds, as well as giving herbal medicines. There were some jobs for women outside the home as well, these included ale-wife, baker and even ironmonger.

Common women had more freedom to choose their partner than noble women, and they married later at around twenty-five, when they were ready to set up home on their own.

English customs were very free and easy compared to most countries' and women profited from this. It was said to be a paradise for married women. There was very little jealousy, everybody kissed everybody else and even a male guest was expected to kiss his hostess on the mouth. Foreigners loved it. Here are some other things which struck them about Englishwomen:

They ride forth alone and are as skilful and firm in the saddle as a man.

At banquets ladies are shown the greatest honour, being placed at the top end of the table and served first.

Even ladies of distinction drink wine in taverns.

They often drive out by coach dressed in fine clothes, and men must put up with such ways.

THE ALMOST KINGS OF ENGLAND

Elizabeth never believed that women were equal to men, but she was still the freest of all the women in her kingdom. Not only did she curse and swear and ride after the hunt like a man, she also never got married. Instead, she used her availablity for marriage as a lure to make other governments do what she wanted.

There were four
men who
thought they
had a chance
of marrying her:

1. Lord Thomas Seymour
2. King Philip of Spain
3. Robert Dudley, Earl of Leicester
4. Francis, Duke of Alencon, a French royal

Nobody believed Elizabeth when she first said that she was married to England, but in actual fact she meant it. Which was tough on Dudley and the other would-be kings of England.

Quite a contrast to her cousin, Mary Queen of Scots, who married three times...

OFF WITH HER HEAD!

SCOTTISH MARY AND THE MULTIPLE MURDERS

There were two difficult Marys in Elizabeth's life and they were both relations:

MARY NO 1
Bloody Queen Mary, Elizabeth's sister, who died in 1558.

MARY NO 2
Mary Queen of Scots, Elizabeth's cousin. Mary Queen of Scots was among Elizabeth's nearest relatives and would succeed to the throne if Elizabeth died.

Scotland was always a headache for Elizabeth, and Mary Queen of Scots was a special headache. Mary was a very tall, beautiful woman, who liked speaking French. She had been brought up in France and had married the heir to the French throne when she was sixteen, returning to Scotland after he died. Scotland always seemed like a foreign country to her.

The Scotland that Mary returned to was sometimes

called 'the arse of the world'. The climate was awful, the nobles were rough and dressed like commoners, not many people spoke French – and worst of all it was full of Puritans.

WHO WANTS MY OLD BOYFRIEND?

PROBLEM:

Every Englishman knew that Catholics would love to get rid of Elizabeth and put good Catholic Mary Queen of Scots on the throne of England.

ELIZABETH'S SOLUTION:

Mary should marry Dashing Dudley, a Protestant English nobleman. This was an odd idea; after all, Dudley was Elizabeth's favourite courtier and everyone thought he was her lover as well (which he may have been). Why would Mary marry one of Elizabeth's cast-offs when he wasn't even royal?

Things would all have been a lot simpler if one of the two queens had been a man, then they could have married each other.

PURELY FOR PURITANS

Elizabeth started the Church of England in 1559 to stop English Protestants and Catholics fighting each other. It was mildly Protestant. Puritans were extreme Protestants; they were in the Church of England, but they weren't happy about it, because it wasn't strict enough for them.

Scottish Puritans were much more influential than English ones. Many top Scottish noblemen were Puritans, and the Puritan Scottish organisation, known as the Congregation, was a powerful force in the land. But the Scottish Puritans weren't happy either.

Here are some things Puritans didn't like:

STATUES AND PAINTINGS IN CHURCHES

MAKING THE SIGN OF THE CROSS

BISHOPS

WEDDING RINGS

MINISTERS DRINKING AND GAMBLING

COLOURFUL CLOTHES

DANCING

WELL DARN IT, DARNLEY!

Alright, so Mary wouldn't marry Dudley, or Dudley wouldn't marry Mary. Elizabeth, or at least her ministers, had another good-looking English nobleman up her sleeve. The new noble was a young, handsome, six-foot-something charmer who was four years younger than Mary. He was called Lord Darnley, he was taller than Mary, and even though he was a Catholic he was ideal – so it was a pity that his personality turned out to be so much worse than his looks.

Darnley came to visit and Mary fell madly in love with him. Even though her Protestant Scottish lords hated him, and Elizabeth changed her mind about him (Elizabeth was always changing her mind) Mary married Darnley anyway. The ceremony took place on 29th July, 1565.

MURDER NO 1
DAVID RIZZIO, UGLY BUT NOT UGLY ENOUGH

Darnley was handsome, but Mary soon discovered that he was also a nasty drunk brute. He was sometimes so rude that he made her cry. She started to hate him...

Mary turned for company to her secretary, David Rizzio. Rizzio was small and ugly but he was a good singer and was fun to talk to. There is no reason to believe that Mary and Rizzio were lovers, but devilish Darnley came to believe that they were.

On Saturday 9th March 1566 Mary was holding a small supper party in her private rooms. The guests were a few close friends including Rizzio. Suddenly Darnley appeared through a private door. He was followed shortly after by a friend, wearing a helmet and with his armour showing beneath his gown, and by some other ruffians. Rizzio clung to Mary's dress but his fingers were forced open and he was dragged away to be stabbed to death with over fifty dagger wounds.

Mary never forgave Darnley and she suspected that Darnley had wanted to kill her as well.

MURDER NO 2
DARNLEY AND THE BIG BANG

Darnley went from bad to worse. He was out drinking almost every night. Mary turned for help to a Protestant Scottish nobleman, the Earl of Bothwell. Bothwell and most other Scottish nobles were sick and tired of Darnley.

Then Darnley fell ill. He was put to bed in a house on the outskirts of Edinburgh. At two o'clock in the morning of Sunday 9th February the quiet of the Edinburgh suburbs was shattered by a gigantic explosion in the house where Darnley was staying. His body was thrown right out of the house into the garden, and the house itself was smashed into a pile of rubble.

The explosion had been planned by Bothwell and a group of noblemen to cover up the fact that they had murdered Darnley, by destroying the evidence. The plot failed in so far as Darnley's body was thrown clear and it was obvious that he had been strangled, but at least he was well and truly dead.

Most people thought that Mary was involved in the plan to murder her horrible husband.

MARRIAGE NO 3
BOTHWELL BREAKS IT OFF

Mary made a big mistake in trusting Bothwell. He now took her away by force and made her marry him. She didn't love him – among other things he was too short. But the fact that they got married made people even more sure that she had helped in the murder of Darnley. The other nobles now turned on Bothwell. Soon he had to flee the country and poor Mary fell into the power of his enemies. They locked her up in a castle in the middle of Lochleven. When at last she escaped, in a boat, disguised as a serving woman, she had no friends left in Scotland. She fled to England leaving behind her son, the future King James of England and Scotland, and threw herself on the mercy of her cousin Elizabeth.

WHATA LOTA PLOTS

So now Mary, the Catholic heir to the throne of England, was in England. Catholics of all kinds saw their chance to get rid of Protestant Elizabeth and to turn the country Catholic. Elizabeth kept Mary under guard in the north of England, but even so, Mary still became the focus for a series of plots against Elizabeth.

THE THROCKMORTON PLOT

Francis Throckmorton planned for an invasion of England by Spain, a Catholic country, to put Mary on the throne. In 1583 he was caught and horribly tortured. He gave away the names of his fellow conspirators before being executed.

ALRIGHT, THROCKMORTON, START TALKING.

THE RIDOLFI PLOT

Roberto Ridolfi was an Italian banker and keen Catholic. He planned a Catholic invasion of England to put Mary on the throne. The plot was discovered by Elizabeth's secret service and the conspirators were caught – except Ridolfi, who was out of the country.

THE BABINGTON PLOT

Babington was a rich young English Catholic who planned to kill Elizabeth and put Mary on the throne. Letters passed back and forth between Mary and the conspirators in water-proof leather packets hidden in beer barrels. Elizabeth's secret service found out about the plot and decoded the letters. Babington went into hiding but was captured by Elizabeth's agents.

Elizabeth had had enough. It was clear from the letters in Babington's beer barrel that Mary had planned to have her murdered. Mary was tried by Elizabeth's ministers at Fotheringhay Castle in Northamptonshire and sentenced to death. Elizabeth was always terrible at making decisions, but finally she signed the warrant for Mary's execution.

On the 8th February 1587 Mary walked into the great hall at Fotheringhay. She had grown fat, but she was still elegantly dressed in a black satin dress. It took two blows of the axe to cut off her head. Afterwards the executioner picked up the head by its red-brown hair, but as he did so the head fell to the floor. The hair in his hand was a wig and Mary's real hair on the head which rolled on the floor was grey. Mary's lips continued to move for a quarter of an hour after her head was chopped off.

WORKERS AND SHIRKERS

GIZZA JOB, LIZ!

BUT FIRST – MIND THAT SLIPPER!

Elizabethan England was young and frisky. As much as half of the population was under twenty, and it was not easy to control them. On all important matters, such as the execution of Mary Queen of Scots, Elizabeth made the final decision, but she ruled though her Council of Ministers.

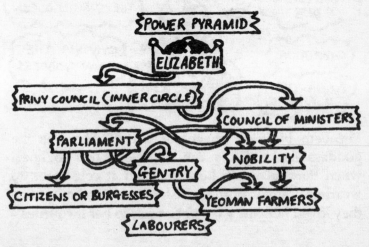

POWER PYRAMID

ELIZABETH

PRIVY COUNCIL (INNER CIRCLE)

COUNCIL OF MINISTERS

PARLIAMENT

NOBILITY

GENTRY

CITIZENS OR BURGESSES

YEOMAN FARMERS

LABOURERS

61

Elizabeth was not an easy person to work for. Ministers had to be ready to be slapped in the face or have a slipper thrown at them. She was bossy, swore a lot, laughed loudly and marched round the room while she was talking, generally behaving in a very unlady-like way for the time.

Her ministers had to work very hard, but if they asked her for help they were either ignored or made fun of. Worst of all she could never make up her mind on important decisions. Ministers used to rush away with papers after she had signed them, before she could change her mind.

Finally, if one of their policies was successful, they had to make sure that Elizabeth got all the credit – and if things went wrong they had to take the blame. She used to make them really upset: 'God's wounds! This is to serve a base, bastard, pissing kitchen woman!' as one of them said.

Elizabeth built an image for herself. She was the goddess-like virgin queen. Everyone had to kneel when they talked to her. The men at court took to wearing a small portrait of her to show how much they loved her. She gave pet names to her favourites.

CATALOGUE OF COURTIERS...

WILLIAM CECIL, BARON BURGHLEY, 1520-98 HER 'SPIRIT' His mother ran a wine shop. He became the most important man in the country for most of Elizabeth's reign, as principle Secretary of State. She grew very fond of him. When he was weak and dying she fed him with a spoon.

ROBERT CECIL, c1563-1612 Son of William Cecil. He took over his father's job when his father was too old. He had a slight hunchback. His quiet, businesslike manner disguised a love of gambling and jolly dinner parties where his pet parrot would jump up and down on the table.

THE EARL OF LEICESTER (DASHING ROBERT DUDLEY) c1532-88 HER 'EYES' Leicester was Cecil's main opponent in the Council of Ministers. He was also Elizabeth's closest friend.

SIR FRANCIS WALSINGHAM, c1532-90 'THE MOOR'  **(BECAUSE OF HIS DARK COLOURING)** Elizabeth's private secretary and head of her secret service, a bit of a Puritan.

 Moors were Muslims who lived in Spain. They were dark-skinned and came originally from Africa.

Sir Walter Raleigh, 1554-1618

A dashing, handsome explorer and writer who founded the colony of Virginia. He was imprisoned after Elizabeth died, then was released briefly to look for gold in America, but was beheaded when he returned empty-handed. He became known as the last of the Elizabethans.

Robert Devereux, 2nd Earl of Essex, c1566-1601

More about him later.

Made in England

Elizabeth was careful with money and England in the sixteenth century was getting rich. At the start of Elizabeth's reign, guns were imported from abroad. By the end of it foreigners were buying guns from England.

Floods of Protestant refugees poured into the country from the Continent, but Europe's loss was England's gain. They brought with them skills like silk weaving, linen weaving, glass making, engraving and printing.

Miners were brought over from Germany, so that the English could learn their secrets. Cotton was introduced by merchants trading with Turkey. By 1565 steel was being produced in Kent. A wire-works was set up in the grounds of ruined Tintern Abbey. It employed more than a hundred people.

WHATA LOTA SQUATTERS

Wool was England's biggest export. There were three sheep to each person in the country. The Duke of Norfolk alone owned 16,800. Every year, over 100,000 woollen clothes were sent abroad to Antwerp.

There was a shortage of work in the countryside because so many sheep were reared, and sheep don't need much looking after. This was fine for those who had some land, but not so good for landless labourers.

Families driven from their jobs by the abundance of sheep might put up simple shacks on waste land at night. They had to build their shacks quickly; they had the right to stay if smoke could be seen rising from a hole in the roof by morning. Such families were horribly poor. When John Warde, a Worcester labourer, died in 1608 all he left behind him were his clothes, his working tools, and a few sticks of furniture, with a total value of less than £3.

RAGGED REBELS

An army of around 20,000 ragged vagabonds festered at the bottom of Tudor society. These were people with no legal way of making a living in the place where they were born. Mostly they were labourers who had lost their jobs because of all the sheep, but there were others as well:

○ In every town there was a mob of the very poor. They might be vagabonds from the country, soldiers with no war to fight, masterless people or general misfits.

○ There were bands of gypsies on the loose, known as gypsies because they were thought to have come from Egypt. They had dark skin and wore piles of rags and rich clothes all mixed up and big gold-embroidered head-coverings. They were thought to be expert thieves and fortune-tellers.

There were laws, dating from Henry VIII's time, to make all these 'sturdy beggars' stay at home, where they were meant to be looked after by the overseer of the poor, and there were specially strict laws for gypsies. But many vagabonds took to a life of crime, to avoid a life of poverty in their home town or village.

STOP THIEF!

It was a hard job keeping control in the towns and villages. The local court was run by a Justice of the

Peace, (JP), normally a local gentleman. He appointed constables from the local yeomen or citizens. It was their job to help the JP and to raise a 'hue and cry' after a robbery or attack. In a hue and cry everyone was meant to chase after the criminal.

There were plenty of crimes apart from robbery to keep the constables busy:

Being a vagabond

Hanging around
ale-houses

Parsons who diced and swore

Being sick in church

Drinking during
service time

Parent-beating (wife-
beating was not a crime)

Incest and bigamy

All-round
evil-living

In addition the Welsh were
known for carrying off widows.

DEVIL'S DICTIONARY

JARKMEN
forged licences to beg and other
documents, known as gybes.

FRATERS
pretended to be
collecting money
for charity.

DOXIES
were the
prostitutes and
the womenfolk
of criminals.

CURTSEY MEN
made out they were gentry
fallen on hard times.

DELLS
were young girls who
were not yet doxies.

PATRICOS OR HEDGE-PRIESTS
performed marriages. They
weren't real priests; the couple
could separate by shaking hands
over any dead animal which they
happened to pass in the road.

HEDGE-CREEPERS
were robbers who
hid in hedges.

COUNTERFEIT CRANKS *pretended to be ill.*

UPRIGHT MEN *(they were also be known as rufflers) were the leaders of robber gangs.*

PRIGGERS OF PRANCERS *were horse thieves.*

NIPS *cut purses with a knife and a 'horn thumb'.*

KINCHIN COES *were little boys who were brought up to steal.*

KINCHIN MORTS *were little girls who were brought up to steal.*

WHIP-JACKS *pretended to be shipwrecked sailors.*

PALLIARDS *begged by showing off scars which had been made revolting with arsenic and ratsbane, or perhaps a mixture of crowfoot, spearwort and salt.*

Painful Punishments

Rogues who were caught and sentenced were unlikely to spend long in prison. The Tudors preferred other punishments and also executed about eight hundred people a year.

Thieves might be burned through the ears.

People who held unconventional religious views were burned to death, as heretics.

Vagabonds were branded with red hot irons and could be whipped back to their home parishes.

Thieves might have their hands or some other bit chopped off.

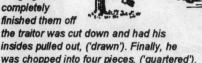

Traitors were 'hung, drawn and quartered'. Before the hanging had completely finished them off the traitor was cut down and had his insides pulled out, ('drawn'). Finally, he was chopped into four pieces, ('quartered').

Thieves were often put in the stocks or the pillory. The pillory was worse than the stocks because in the pillory the hands were held and the victim could not defend his face from anything thrown at him. Sometimes his ears were nailed to the wood so that he couldn't look down. If hard objects were thrown the victim might die.

Women, who'd been thought to have committed a misdemeanor could be forced to walk around in a sheet.

Noblemen were beheaded.

Poisoners might be boiled to death in lead or water.

SPLUPHGUMPF

In London prostitutes might be pulled behind a boat in the Thames.

Women were often ducked in a ducking stool for misdemeanors like adultery. If the people doing the ducking were feeling nasty, this could be a dangerous punishment, and some women drowned.

Women could be forced to wear a scold's bridle if they were thought to nag their husbands or to gossip too much.

LONDON AND LOUTS HARD BARDS

The most important place for Elizabeth to control was London. About 200,000 people lived there, most of them Protestant. It was by far the richest city but it was not a peaceful place. No one went out at night on their own if they could avoid it and if they had to, they took a sword and lantern to defend themselves against the low-life lying in wait. Fights between neighbours often ended with swords being drawn.

Londoners had no time for foreigners, who were scoffed at and teased on the streets. Schoolboys were specially fond of shouting insults or throwing things at them.

Sometimes anti-foreigner feeling blew up into a full scale riot, such as 'Evil Mayday' in 1517 – called evil because thirteen young rioters were hanged, not because of what was done to any foreigners.

The houses were packed in like sardines and so were the people inside them. One medium-sized house in Dowgate housed eleven married couples and fifteen single people!

At five o'clock each morning carts loaded with food would rumble in from nearby towns and villages. In 1581, 2,100 horses were counted travelling on just one road. With so many people packed into such a small space there were bound to be terrible traffic problems, and the number of coaches  and carts made the streets dangerous to walk on. Agressive wandering pigs were another serious danger, sometimes even killing children.

Scavengers and dust carts tried to keep the streets clean, but there weren't enough to keep the dirt at bay.

 Coaches were a new form of transport called after Kotze in Hungary, where they were first made.

The crowded houses were infested with rats and there was a lack of clean water, even after 1572 when a German called Peter Morris designed a pump to take water from the Thames. It was powered by a waterwheel which was turned by the rush of water between one of the arches of London Bridge. At its first demonstration it shot a plume of water right over a church.

> Step up for my terrific tour of Tudor London!

TUDOR TOURISTS

London was more famous than England itself. An English merchant at the Persian court in 1568 reported that no one there had heard of England, but everyone had heard of London. There was a tourist circuit for foreigners.

LONDON BRIDGE was a favourite with its twenty stone arches, lined with shops and houses on both sides. It had the added attraction of the rotting heads of traitors stuck on poles above the drawbridge.

THE TOWER OF LONDON
was another favourite,
being the place where the
traitors lost their heads in
the first place. It also had its
famous armoury and a
small zoo of wild animals.

ST PAUL'S CATHEDRAL
towered above Tudor London. It
was a popular meeting place
where people went to hire
servants, show off new clothes
or look at the job advertisements
pasted on the pillars.

WESTMINSTER ABBEY
with its royal tombs
was always
popular.

THE ROYAL EXCHANGE
in Cornhill was opened
in 1571 by Elizabeth. It
was where merchants
went to do deals.

ORDINARY AFTERNOONS

Those with the time and the money would often take their dinner in an 'ordinary' or pub. Ordinaries were very popular. They were used for eating, drinking, talking, card-playing, and dice among other things. Here's some sarcastic advice to a brash young gallant, or man of fashion, on how to show off in an ordinary:

> Draw out your tobacco box just when
> the meat comes to the board, rise in the
> middle of the meal and ask for a 'close stool'
> (a kind of chamber pot), invite a friend to
> join you while you sit on the stool
> in the withdrawing room (toilet).

TIME FOR ANOTHER?

Since lunch started around twelve o'clock there was plenty of time for a young gallant and his friends to drink beer or wine before finishing the meal at around two. Then it was time for business or entertainment. What could be better than to take a boat across the river to the leisure area on the other side, and maybe go to a play or some other entertainment? The boats often had cushions on their seats and awnings above to protect their passengers from the sun and rain.

The South Bank was the best place to go for bull and bear baiting, and for the new theatres.

The South Bank was outside the city limits, and therefore beyond the reach of the city government. The city government was full of Puritans who thought that plays were the work of the devil. Perhaps they were right – there were also five prisons on the South Bank: the King's Bench, Marshalsea, White Lion, Counter and Clink.

Bear baiting was popular but plays were the height of fashion. As many as 15,000 people per week went to the theatre. Plays started at two o'clock because there was no artificial light for night-time performances.

TOP TUDOR THEATRES

 THE THEATRE, built 1576, knocked down in 1597 and materials used to build the Globe.

 THE GLOBE, first built 1599, burned down 1613 and rebuilt 1614 .

 THE FORTUNE, built 1600, burned down 1621 and rebuilt 1623.

Performances were also given in the courtyards of inns and at 'private' theatres, which were used by the upper classes.

 The Globe has recently been rebuilt in almost exactly the same position as the original theatre on the South Bank of the Thames using exactly the same Elizabethan building materials of timber frame and thatched roof.

ELIZABETHAN THEATRE

Elizabethans liked their plays to have lots of noise and special effects.

AUDIENCES OF THREE THOUSAND WERE NOT UNCOMMON.

UNPOPULAR PLAYS MIGHT BE HISSED AT HOOTED AND 'PIPPIN-PELTED' FROM THE STAGE.

MISTS AND FOGS FROM TRAP DOORS

There was often bear-baiting or other animal entertainments before and after plays.

THE ACTOR FACTOR

Actors were known for being heavy-drinking brawlers, boasters, lovers and ruffians. A law of 1572 said that all actors were rogues and vagabonds if they did not belong to an established company run by a lord or high-up person. This meant that they could be branded with a V for vagabond and whipped back to their native town or village.

But professional actors worked hard for their money. One company, the Admiral's Men, put on sixty-two different plays between 1599 and 1600. The Admiral's Men and the Chamberlain's Men, in which Shakespeare was a shareholder, were the two main companies of actors.

Elizabeth and her courtiers loved watching plays as much as everyone else. Shakespeare's company often had to give their first performance of a new work before the royal court.

MORRIS MARATHON
William Kempe, a clown
from Shakespeare's
company, did a hundred
mile solo morris dance from
Norwich to London, then
wrote a book about it.

TOP TUDOR WRITERS

Some of the greatest
English writers ever
flourished during
Elizabeth's
reign:

EDMUND SPENSER c1552-99,

He was a friend of Sir Philip Sidney. Among
other poems, he wrote the *Faerie Queen* which
praises Elizabeth.

SIR PHILIP SIDNEY 1554-86

An aristocrat, poet, Protestant and soldier. He
died at the battle of Zutphen in the
Netherlands, having given his own water to a
soldier who was dying beside him.

THOMAS KYD 1558-94

Tom Kyd was the son of a scrivener (someone
who copied documents). He was arrested and
tortured for treason in 1593. His most famous
play was *The Spanish Tragedy*. Died in debt.

CHRISTOPHER MARLOWE 1564-93

The son of a shoemaker, he was the greatest
playwright after Shakespeare. He worked for
the secret service, was accused of atheism, and
died from a stab wound in the eye in Deptford.

WILLIAM SHAKESPEARE 1564-1616

William was the son of a Stratford glover, who married an older woman then made his way to London to become the most famous writer of all time. A rumour started by an unfriendly clergyman said that Shakespeare indulged in heavy drinking with Ben Jonson shortly before his death.

BEN JONSON 1573- 1637

Ben Jonson was apprenticed to a bricklayer, fought as a soldier, became poet-laureat, was sentenced for the murder of one of his fellow actors, but set free by pleading 'benefit of clergy' . He may have worked for the secret service.

FRANCIS BEAUMONT 1584-1616 AND
JOHN FLETCHER 1579-1625

This pair were more upper-class than the other playwrights of the period. They shared the writing of their plays. The early ones were performed by Shakespeare's company.

It was a good time to be a writer, but the government kept a strict control on what was published. Before plays were allowed to be staged each had to be passed by the Lord Chamberlain. Nothing critical of the government was allowed.

If a convict could prove that he could read, he was said to be technically a clergyman and could only be tried by church courts. This strange law dated back to the Middle Ages when only priests could read and write.

LOADS OF LOOT

POSH PIRATES ON THE SEVEN SEAS

Elizabeth's reign wasn't just a golden age for writers. It was a golden age for sailors and explorers as well. When she came to the throne, England was a backward island on the edge of Europe, and English people never travelled much further than France or Italy. With Elizabeth's encouragement Englishmen sailed right round the world, penetrating the icy seas of Russia and the warm seas of Africa, and English travellers roamed across Asia and Turkey.

IT'S DAYLIGHT ROBBERY!

There was not much difference between explorers and pirates. If you robbed for the Queen you were a hero!

HOW TO BE A ROBBER-HERO:

1. Get yourself a ship
2. Rob Spaniards

Privateers were pirates who were licensed to attack enemy shipping (which usually meant the Catholic Spanish), so English privateering was legal - at least as far as Elizabeth was concerned. The Spanish didn't agree of course.

Privateering was gambling for high stakes. It could be profitable, but it was also very, very risky. The financial backers often lost their money, and many sailors lost their lives.

ANYONE FOR RAT?

Tudor sailors were as tough as pickled Protestants, which is in fact exactly what they were. They ate and slept in tiny 'messes' of four or five sailors behind canvass screens. They shared the space with another mess of the same number, sleeping and eating while the other mess was working.

Standard daily rations per mess included twenty-five pints of beer. The beer often used to run out or become too disgusting to swallow. Sailors on long voyages spoke of eating candles and rats, of cutting up leather and boiling it for dinner and of holding their noses while they drank stinking water from the pump.

The sailors died like flies from all kinds of diseases like malaria and yellow fever, but the worst plague of all was scurvy, caused by a lack of vitamin C, contained in fresh fruit and vegetables. Scurvy was reckoned to have killed more than a thousand sailors a year at the time.

A VICTIM OF SCURVY

BLEEDING GUMS

ACHING JOINTS

BOW LEGS

The standard large ship for privateers was the galleon. Galleons were quite slim, with a section which jutted out at the front, called the beakhead. In time this became the 'heads' or toilet.

The ships were built by eye. Only the length of the biggest timbers was measured. First the backbone or 'keel' was laid down, this was a huge timber which ran the length of the bottom of the ship, then the ship was built up round it. To curve the planks, they were laid on hot coals and water was sloshed over them while they were bent into shape.

Ballast was laid on planks at the bottom of each ship to keep it upright.

The ballast was normally heavy stones. The galley or cooking space was a brick firebox, usually set in the middle of the ballast area among the rat droppings and smelly stink from the ballast and the bilge water, which collected at the bottom of the ship.

Ships' outer timbers were always under attack from the dreaded teredo worm, which lives in the sea and burrows into wood. Spaniards coated their ships in lime, sulphur and fish oil in an effort to protect them from the worm. The English preferred tar mixed with goat-hair. Neither of these mixtures was much use. Every three months or so ships had to be 'careened'. This meant scraping the hull free of barnacles and other sea creatures and then re-coating it. They sometimes tried to scorch the hull with fire, which could be disastrous.

Sails were huge baggy things made of flax. They were hung from wide wooden 'yardarms', which were often tipped with iron sickles to rip enemy rigging. Galleons weren't very fast, and if a ship wanted to put on speed, the sails were wetted to make them more taut. Maximum speed with a scraped bottom and wet sails was no more than about six mph (10 kph).

The best thing to do in a gale was to run for the nearest port. If that wasn't possible, the captain would order that all the sails be lowered to the deck, or 'struck'. They lowered every thing except the bottom stumps of the masts and possibly one sail at the front or 'bows'. Then they swung the ship round so that it faced into the crashing waves and stayed like that until the storm blew over.

The rudder was moved with ropes or a lever. But the really big problem was knowing where you were in the first place...

How to get there

If they were sailing near to the coast, sailors could steer by local knowledge such as knowing the depth of the sea in different places. In the middle of the ocean things were far more difficult. To help them find their way around, sailors had four main instruments:

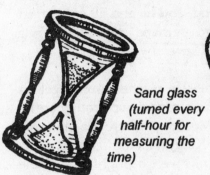

Sand glass (turned every half-hour for measuring the time)

Magnetic compass

The 'log', a wooden board attached to a line which was thrown over the side to measure the speed of the ship. The line was allowed to run out in its own time, and the time it took to run out to its full length was measured.

Sea Astrolabe. This was for measuring the height of the sun at noon. Sailors had books which told them how high the sun should be in different latitudes (positions north or south) at different times of year. The astrolabe was hung up on the deck while a sailor stood on the rolling deck and tried to see the sun through a tiny hole.

Great Adventure No.1
Richard Chancellor and the Six Gallon Bowls

On 10th May 1553 Sir Hugh Willoughby set sail from London to search for a sea route right around the north of Europe and Asia to China. His  second-in-command was Richard Chancellor of Bristol. Off the coast of Norway the two men were separated in a terrible storm. Willoughby's ship ended up stuck in ice off Lapland, and he and all of his men died of scurvy, cold and perhaps starvation. Their frozen bodies were found several years later.

Chancellor went on alone. He reached Archangel on the shore of the White Sea before winter. From there he travelled overland to Moscow, where he met the barbaric Russian Tsar, or King, Ivan the Terrible, at his splendid court where drinks were brought to the table in six-gallon (nearly twenty-eight litre) silver bowls. This was the start of trade between Russia and England, and on Chancellor's return to England the Muscovy Company was set up.

Great Adventure No.2
Anthony Jenkinson and the Horse-meat Merchants

Anthony Jenkinson was chief agent of the Muscovy Company, based in Moscow. In 1558 he set off from Moscow, hoping to reach the Middle East

overland from the North. He travelled 1,800 miles down the Volga, sailed across the Caspian Sea to Turkestan, then hitched up with a camel-train to Bokhara. Jenkinson described how the Tartar nomads ate horse flesh and loved to get drunk on fermented mare's milk. At one stage he had to fight a running battle with robbers for four days and nights in the middle of a desert with no water to drink.

Jenkinson returned to Moscow from Astrakhan with an armed company of Tartar ambassadors and dined with the Tsar of Russia on the 2nd September, his long journey over at last. He reported that the people of Central Asia were too savage to bother with.

GREAT ADVENTURE No.3
SIR JOHN HAWKINS AND THE LEAKY LUBECK

In October 1567 Sir John Hawkins set sail from Plymouth with six ships although his flagship, the *Jesus of Lubeck*, leaked like a sieve. Along the west  coast of Africa, they helped an African king in a local war and took some prisoners to sell as slaves in South America.

Having sold his slaves, Hawkins was battered by a massive storm in the Caribbean, and the *Jesus of Lubeck* came apart at the seams. He limped to shelter in the port of San Juan de Ulua.

Then unluckily the Spanish fleet arrived. This posed a problem, because the Pope (who claimed to get his power directly from God) had given half the world outside Europe to Catholic Spain and the other half to Catholic Portugal, and the Spaniards did not want Protestants like Hawkins to trade in their patch.

Hawkins let them enter the port, and that night the treacherous Spaniards attacked. Out of around four hundred English sailors, half survived the fight, including Hawkins and his young follower, Francis Drake, but half of these survivors had to be left on the coast of South America due to lack of food and water. There they were captured by the Spanish, and one was later burned to death in Seville market-place.

GREAT ADVENTURE No.4
MARTIN FROBISHER AND THE ANGRY INUIT

The English hoped to find a quick sea passage around the north of America to China. Frobisher was a tough sea-dog from Yorkshire who set out in June 1576, sailing north-west past the massive icebergs and mountains of Greenland. For months he wandered in the freezing, gloomy waters around Baffin Island and beyond, searching for a route through, but without success.

They met Eskimos, or Inuit as they are now sometimes called. Frobisher was very strong. Wanting a captive to take back to England, he lifted an Inuit, canoe and all, into his ship, the *Gabriel*. The Inuit was so angry that he bit his tongue in two, but survived with half a tongue – only to die of a common cold on the way to England.

Frobisher failed to find the North-West Passage on this or two more voyages. But he did bring back a lump of 'fools' gold' or pyrites, which looks like gold, starting a mini gold-rush, in which many people, including Elizabeth, lost money.

GREAT ADVENTURE NO.5
FRANCIS DRAKE'S VOYAGE ROUND THE WORLD

In 1577, Francis Drake, already a top Tudor sea-dog, sailed from Plymouth with a fleet of five ships. Among his financial backers was Elizabeth herself. They sailed across the Atlantic to South America. Fearing a mutiny among his gentlemen sailors, he beheaded the leader, and for the rest of the voyage the gentlemen were treated exactly equally with the common sailors.

In August 1578 they rounded the Straits of Magellan and entered the Pacific, where they started on an orgy of looting among Spanish ships and settlements along the west coast of South America, sailing north as far as modern California.

Then they struck out across the Pacific and sailed back to England via India and Africa, reaching Plymouth in September 1580. They had taken so much loot that Drake's flagship, the *Golden Hind*, was said to be ballasted with treasure. The total value of their haul was about £600,000, a huge fortune in those days, of which Elizabeth got the lion's share.

Of 160 men who set out, 59 returned, the rest died. Drake was not a cruel man; far fewer Spaniards than Englishmen died during his adventures.

GREAT ADVENTURE No.6
RALPH FITCH AND THE OIL POOLS

Ralph Fitch and his friend, John Newbury, sailed from Falmouth to Tripoli in Syria in 1583. From there they travelled by camel and boat down the river Euphrates to Babylon. They were the first Englishmen to see Middle East oil, where it bubbled up in squelchy black pools south of Babylon. Arabs said the pools were the mouth of hell. From Babylon they took a ship to India and made it to the court of the Great Mogul.

At this point Newbury turned for home, but Fitch went on. He sailed down the river Ganges to Bengal, across the across the Bay of Bengal to Burma, then to Siam (modern Thailand) and from there to Malaya, which was the furthest he got.

When he arrived back in England eight years later, he found that he had been presumed dead and his belongings had been given to his relatives.

GREAT ADVENTURE NO.7
THOMAS CAVENDISH AND THE PLAGUE OF MAGGOTS

Thomas Cavendish was an adventurer from Suffolk who in 1586 had copied Drake's voyage round the world. He tried it again in 1591, sailing from Plymouth with five ships – with 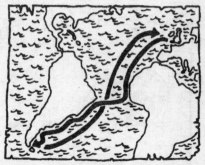 disastrous results. The officers quarrelled, the weather was awful, food was short, and the ships were rotten.

Soon they were starving. Some men were too weak to move and lice as big as beans bred in their skin. In the Straits of Magellan they killed some penguins to eat but the birds rotted, breeding a plague of maggots which ate into the flesh of the sailors and bit like mosquitos. They were forced to turn back.

Finally they got scurvy. Their ankles swelled, and then their chests so that they were unable to breath easily, and finally their genitals swelled up. Some went mad and died in horrible pain. Out of a crew of ninety-one, five were left in a fit shape to sail the ship back to Ireland, eleven were too sick, and the rest were dead.

A COMPANY OF COMPANIES

The Turkey or Levant Company, formed 1581, traded across the Mediterranean with Constantinople. Their ships risked capture and slavery by the Barbary pirates, whose slave-powered galleys lurked in the warm waters.

Trading and privateering were two sides of the same coin. All Elizabethan merchants were happy to do a bit of privateering on the side, as they fanned out across the world in search of trade and plunder. They invented the 'joint stock company' whereby groups of merchants clubbed together to put up the money for expeditions and to share the risk. Here are some of the main companies:

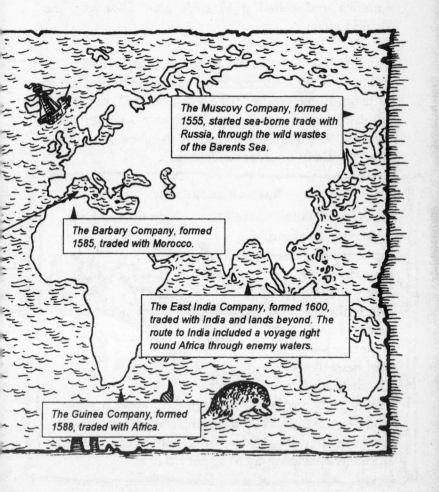

The Muscovy Company, formed 1555, started sea-borne trade with Russia, through the wild wastes of the Barents Sea.

The Barbary Company, formed 1585, traded with Morocco.

The East India Company, formed 1600, traded with India and lands beyond. The route to India included a voyage right round Africa through enemy waters.

The Guinea Company, formed 1588, traded with Africa.

WELL TRIED, WALTER!

Merchants made money by trading with other countries, but it was easier and safer to trade with your own people, like the Spanish did with their colonies in South America.

Handsome dandy Sir Walter Raleigh had a plan to start an English colony. He picked a spot in North America and called it Virginia after Elizabeth, the Virgin Queen.

The first colonists set out in seven ships in 1585. The colony was not a success and a year later they asked to be taken home. Walter tried again in 1587, but it was not until 1607 that a successful colony was planted in Virginia. The capital of Virginia is called Jamestown after Elizabeth's successor, James I.

RALEIGH SMOKE FACT

Sir Walter Raleigh started the fashion for smoking tobacco in England.
Elizabeth discussed his plans for Virginia with him while he puffed away, sometimes she had a puff herself.
Elizabethans

thought tobacco smoke was good for you because it made you cough. They thought all the horrid black stuff that they coughed up was there already, and the smoke was helping them to get rid of it.

ARMADA!

TRY HARDER ARMADA

PHILIP PLANS AN EXPEDITION

○ Philip was leader of the most powerful Catholic empire in the world.

○ Elizabeth was Queen of the most powerful Protestant country in the world.

Philip had a problem and that problem was Elizabeth. His Protestant subjects in the Netherlands were in armed rebellion against his army. As long as the rebels got help from Protestants in England they need never surrender. As long as Elizabeth was Queen of England, England would stay a Protestant country.

So England and Spain were in a state of war or something like it for years. English seamen plundered Spanish shipping, and the Spaniards killed them when they caught them – which wasn't very often. It was all very unsatisfactory.

ENGLEESH PEEG

Something would have to be done...

Philip was very religious. He built a palace called the *Escurial* on a mountain near Madrid. It was like a monastery; through a window in his bedroom he looked directly down on the high altar of the chapel.

Tortured by an illness called gout, he worked day and night at his desk in his lonely palace, on papers which came in from all corners of his vast Empire in Europe and America. It was here at his desk that he decided to invade England, or at least force Elizabeth to stop causing trouble.

The plan was simple: gather a vast fleet of ships in Spain, sail up the English Channel, smashing the English fleet if it got in the way, join up with the Spanish forces in the Netherlands, then ship the entire army across the Channel and invade England, where he hoped that English Catholics would rise up to support him.

What could be simpler...?

THE ARMADA

The Spanish fleet which Philip gathered at Lisbon, Portugal, (then governed by Spain) was called the Armada. It was massive:

ARMADA ARMAMENTS

```
Big warships and merchantmen — 24
Other ships — 106
 Sailors and soldiers — 19,000
 Cannonballs — 125,790
 Guns — 2,431
```

The English fleet was smaller but they had almost the same number of big guns as the Spaniards, and the English ships were easier to steer which meant that they could slip into the best positions for pounding Spanish ships to bits.

The longest range gun of the period was the basilisk, which was up to five metres long and could hurl an eight kilogram ball more than 2.5 kilometres, but it was too big, too heavy and too inaccurate for use at sea. In fact, firing a gun on a heaving ship at sea was like being roaring drunk with a blindfold on; beyond two hundred metres all guns were wildly inaccurate, and if they were fired more than once every five minutes they became red-hot and dangerous to handle.

The English sailors slept below decks on straw mattresses. The Spanish sailors had to sleep outside, whatever the weather, because all the snug places below decks were taken by the soldiers and officers of the invasion force.

Discipline in both navies was strict. Here's a horrible handful of English naval punishments:

Sailors found guilty of murder were roped to the bodies of their victims and thrown overboard.

Men found asleep on watch were given a knife and a jug of beer then tied under the bowsprit . They could choose whether to die slowly of exposure or cut themselves free, fall into the sea, and die quickly.

Thieves were ducked twelve feet below the water then towed ashore behind a boat and left.

Blasphemers   were gagged tightly for an hour until their mouths were all bloody.

The bowsprit was the long piece of wood which jutted diagonally from the bow of the ship.

Blasphemers were people who made fun of religion or generally spoke against it.

GALLANT GALLERY

The English fleet was led by some of the most daring and skilful sailors of all time.

*CHARLES HOWARD
the Lord High Admiral, a brave,
sport-loving nobleman who
couldn't spell. In fact he wasn't
an experienced sailor – at least
until after the Armada. Howard
divided his fleet into four squadrons. One was under his
own command, the other three were:*

*MARTIN FROBISHER,
the brilliant and tough
explorer of the seas
north of America.*

*JOHN HAWKINS
he was the man who
started all the trouble with
Spanish America.*

*FRANCIS DRAKE
(the Vice- Admiral).
Because of his expeditions
against the Spanish, his
name alone was enough
to strike terror into
Spanish hearts.*

Here's some Armada battle scraps I picked up...

Sidonia Stops Corunna Runners – May 1588

Having left Lisbon on 30th May, the dreaded Spanish Armada is reported struck by storms. Spanish Admiral, the Duke of Medina Sidonia, has been forced to put into the port of Corunna, which has been surrounded by soldiers to stop men deserting.

Pirate Spots Spaniards July 29th

Pirate Thomas Fleming was today first to spot the dreaded Spanish Armada off the Scilly Isles. He sped to Plymouth under full sail to warn Vice-Admiral Francis Drake. Drake is reported to have been playing bowls at the time. The English fleet is now leaving harbour, but the wind is against them. Fast one Fleming!

Battle Beacon Warns Britons – Friday July 29th

Following Fleming's news of the Armada, beacons have been lit on high hills across the country, spreading the news and putting bold Britains everywhere on battle alert.

Militia Men on the March – Stop Press!

The Council of War has ordered an army of 20,000 men to gather at Tilbury and bar the road to London, in case Spanish invaders cross from the Netherlands and land in Essex. All over the country our brave boys are getting ready to fight.

The Elizabethan Echo
Circulation 2 million

Channel Battle Hots Up
August 5th 1588

Over the past few days our brave fleet has fought the Armada in a running battle up the English Channel. Being easier to steer, our ships have managed to keep up-wind of the Spaniards, and have sliced up a few slow-coaches.

Spanish Smashed in Calais Carve-Up!
August 8th

In the early hours of this morning English fireships were set adrift among the Spanish fleet cowering off the coast near Calais, where they had failed to meet up with the Spanish army of the Netherlands. Panic stricken Spaniards sliced their ropes and tried to run for it, but the Spanish fleet has been smashed to pieces by our brave boys in the boats.

The Wind's a Winner
August 9th 1588

Due to the strong northward blowing wind up the English Channel, Spanish Admiral Medina Sidonia has decided to slink home by looping north right round Scotland and Ireland with the remains of his fleet.

Losers Limp Home
September 1588

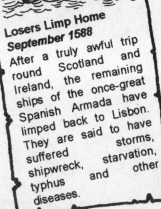

After a truly awful trip round Scotland and Ireland, the remaining ships of the once-great Spanish Armada have limped back to Lisbon. They are said to have suffered storms, shipwreck, starvation, and other typhus diseases.

103

VICTORY FOR THE VIRGIN QUEEN

While the Armada sailed up the English Channel, Elizabeth sailed down the Thames to Tilbury to meet her army. She went for the white, virgin, look when she rode out to review the troops. She wore a white plumed helmet, a white dress with a steel corset over it, rode a white charger, and held a marshal's silver baton.

News of the great victory reached her while she was still at Tilbury and she returned to London, to streets jam-packed with cheering citizens. At fifty-five she was already an old woman by Tudor standards, but she was at the height of her fame and popularity.

TROUBLESOME TOYBOY

HE CLIMBED TOO HIGH

When she was a young queen, Elizabeth was surrounded by men of the same age as her. It was easy to believe them when they said that they loved her. As she grew old, these old friends died or retired and she found herself surrounded by men who were young enough to be her sons – if she had had any.

ONE OUT

Dashing Dudley, Earl of Leicester, grew fat as he grew older and developed pains in the stomach. He died soon after the defeat of the Armada, aged fifty-five. Elizabeth kept his last letter to her in a jewel box in her bedroom.

ONE IN

Handsome twenty-year-old Robert Devereux, Earl of Essex, was the new star at court who replaced Dudley as Elizabeth's favourite. He had shining red-brown hair, bright black eyes, and he was so tall that he marched round the palace leaning forward 'like the neck of a giraffe'.

Elizabeth was mad about him. They often sat up till morning playing cards and other games. She showered him with important jobs and other favours. But he had to be careful not to look at other women, or Elizabeth might get angry. Once he made eyes at Mary Howard, a maid-of-honour, so Elizabeth stole Mary's dress. That evening she stalked into court wearing it, even though it was much too short for her. "How like you my new-fancied suit?" she asked her horrified maids-of-honour.

People liked Essex. He charged through life like a whirlwind in a hurry. He used to shovel down breakfast as quickly as possible then throw on whatever old clothes his servants handed to him. Unfortunately Essex had a personality problem – he was too big for his boots.

Essex wanted to be a famous soldier. This was his undoing. He had already proved he was brave in the Netherlands when he was quite young, but he used to sneak off to join military expeditions. Then if Elizabeth ordered him to come home, he would try to ignore her orders. Essex was always sulking and making up. They had terrible rows when she might slap his ears.

Essex had a seat in the Privy Council where the important government ministers met. He was all for smashing the Spaniards at every opportunity. This brought him up against Secretary of State, William Cecil, the most important man in the country, and William's son, Robert. They were much more cautious and careful than Essex.

WHO'S TOP? *Essex*

In 1596 Elizabeth ordered Essex and Howard, the Lord High Admiral, to share command of an expedition against the Spanish port of Cadiz. 'Lord High Admiral' was senior to any of Essex's job titles, but on the other hand Essex was an earl while Howard was only a baron. Who was more important?

The struggle to be top dog caused a lot of friction. Once, when they had to sign a joint letter to Elizabeth, Essex snatched up his pen and signed so high up on the page that there was no room for Howard to sign above. But cunningly, Howard waited till Essex had left the room then cut out Essex's signature with a knife before posting the letter.

Despite the squabbling, the expedition was a success. Essex lead an attack on the town which even Howard admitted was very brave. They looted lots of treasure and Essex returned to England a hero.

The treasure included a bishop's library, which Essex gave to his friend Thomas Bodley. Bodley later founded the world-famous Bodleian Library in Oxford.

STRANGE THINGS ABOUT IRELAND

Ireland was ruled by England, but it was hard to control, and being Catholic there was always a danger that the Spanish would try to stir up rebellion there - which of course they did.

The English thought that the Irish were barbarians:

 They lived in huts.

 They were infested with lice. The men used to lie on the women's laps while the women picked out the lice with their fingers.

 On feast days they ate half-cooked meat without bread or salt.

 The poor went around completely naked. Even the nobles thought nothing of it. A Bohemian nobleman travelling on Chief O'Cahan's lands in 1601 met sixteen naked women who, 'his eyes being dazzled', led him into their house. They were educated women and spoke Latin with him. Later Chief O'Cahan joined them and he took off his clothes as well.

Irish chiefs sometimes hired warriors from Scotland known as 'gallowglasses'. When Chief Shane O'Neil came to London in 1562, his escort of gallowglasses drew crowds. They had hair to their shoulders and they dyed their vests yellow with urine.

ESSEX TO IRELAND!

The English decided that the Irish were a lost cause. They started to 'plant' colonies of Protestant English families. The settlers thought the Irish were stupid and thought that Ireland was too good a country to have been given by God to such stupid people. The Irish hated the settlers because they were taking the land.

The English governor of Connaught, Sir Richard Bingham, was typical. He thought that the Irish were animals. He took to hanging them, including a one-legged eighty-year-old so it was said. The Irish rose up in a rebellion, led by the Earl of Tyrone, and defeated an English army at Yellow Ford in Armagh. Things were desperate; the English commander suggested using portable racks to torture the Irish into giving away information. Essex pleaded with Elizabeth to be allowed to command a fresh expedition against the rebels. In 1599 she agreed. Essex left for Ireland with an army of 16,000 foot soldiers and 1,300 cavalry.

Tudor armies were full of villains taken from prisons, and other riff-raff. The soldiers' daily rations were bread or biscuit with butter and a gallon of beer. Many foot soldiers had to lug around a musket. These were about a metre long and could fire just one bullet every two minutes. Muskets weighed a ton with all their extras, such as gun-powder and bullets. The English had control of the land around Dublin, known as the *Pale*  . The area under Irish control was called the *Great Irishry*. Essex lead his army outside the Pale but failed to defeat the rebels. Meanwhile his army grew weak through disease.

Elizabeth was angry because Essex had wasted his chance for victory over the rebels. In a desperate attempt to charm her, he left his army in Ireland, sailed back to England against her orders, galloped across the country and burst into her bedroom at Nonsuch Palace spattered with mud, seeing her for the first time with her long grey hair loose. For a moment Elizabeth thought he was going to kill her.

 This where the expression 'beyond the pale' comes from.

110

Essex was banished from court. For over a year he lurked in his London house, which became a centre for all the troublemakers of London. He refused to apologise properly, which was his only chance. Elizabeth heard news that he was plotting against her, but she had to be careful - he was popular with the Puritans.

So she waited.

THE FINAL ACT

In February 1601 Essex tried to start a rebellion. He set out from Essex house with a few followers, shouting to the people to support him, but no one joined in. The citizens kept their doors firmly shut and the rebels trudged on in silence. Realising that his rebellion was doomed, Essex broke out in a cold sweat. He fled by boat up river to his house, where he was surrounded and captured. From then on his fate was sealed.

Essex was beheaded at the Tower of London on 25th February 1601.

GOODBYE ELIZABETH

THE FINAL CHAPTER – ALMOST

By 1601, Elizabeth was starting to feel her age. She knew that Essex had spoken about her 'crooked carcass' behind her back, even when he was pretending to be in love with her. It was after Essex's death that she took to keeping a sword by her bed, and in her fear of murderers sometimes prowled around her private rooms thrusting the sword into the rich wall-hangings.

But she was still the boss. Her perfumed, ear-ringed courtiers still pretended to be in love with her and everyone knelt when they talked to her, unless she told them to stand.

Her clothes were grander than ever, and they had become a little strange. The French ambassador described seeing her in a black taffeta dress which was open to her belly-button. He didn't know where to look when she pulled the dress further apart with her hands.

Elizabeth was old but she was still active. She liked to ride up to fifteen miles in the mornings, with the mane and tail of her horse dyed the same bright orange as her wig. Then at the end of 1602 she got her final illness.

A DEVILISH DICTIONARY OF DREADFUL DISEASES

It was no joke to get sick in Tudor England. They had most of the illnesses we have today – but almost none of the cures...

AGUE

Malaria or *ague* was common in marshy areas like the fens. Infection is from the bite of certain mosquitoes.

BLACK DEATH

Worst of all was the plague or *black death*, which swept across the country in terrible summer epidemics, snuffing out entire streets and villages full of people. The Elizabethans blamed pigs, dogs and cats for carrying it, but not rats – which were the real culprits. The dog population tended to be killed off in times of plague – which must have pleased the rats.

There were two kinds of plague, *pneumonic* and *bubonic*. Pneumonic attacked the lungs and was the most dangerous, *bubonic* caused black bumps to appear on the skin.

GOUT

The upper classes suffered from *gout*, where the big toe becomes swollen and very painful.

GREEN-SICKNESS

Young girls got a sort of anaemia called *green-sickness* because it made their skin look greenish. It is caused by a lack of iron in your diet.

SCURVY

The poor sometimes got *scurvy* from lack of fresh fruit and vegetables at the end of winter. This was the same disease that affected sailors on long voyages. Among other symptoms it caused bleeding gums.

SWEATING SICKNESS

Flu was a new illness, there was a fatal form known as *sweating sickness*.

TYPHUS

Typhus, or goal fever, was carried by lice. If caused headaches, a rash and finally death.

WASTING-SICKNESS

Wasting sickness may have been cancer.

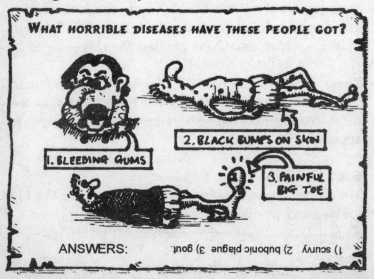

WHAT HORRIBLE DISEASES HAVE THESE PEOPLE GOT?

1. BLEEDING GUMS

2. BLACK BUMPS ON SKIN

3. PAINFUL BIG TOE

ANSWERS: 1) scurvy 2) bubonic plague 3) gout.

DOCTORS DOLITTLE, DABBLE AND RUNNE

Top doctors were in the College of Physicians. They believed that the body was made up of four humours or fluids - black bile, yellow bile, phlegm and blood. They tried to keep the right balance of these humours in their patients by bleeding, diet and purges. Purges made the patient be sick and go to the toilet. Bleeding involved cutting the patient and draining off some blood. Most of the time the doctors didn't have a clue what they were doing.

Here are some typical Tudor diagnoses and descriptions:

He is infected with melancholy and salt phlegm – breeds worms in his nose of stinking sweet and venomous humour.

She was possessed by a sprite which provoked her to kill or drown herself, and bid her cut her throat..the sprite that was in her said he was a sprite of water.

Troubled to perverse humour of gadding: he would go out of door from his wife and friends without any cause..many times they should not see him for a month or more.

WHAT A BLEEDER!

Poxy Liz

*In 1562 Elizabeth had had smallpox, a very
dangerous illness which leaves the patient
scarred by pock marks. Her doctor, Burcot,
suggested an old Arab remedy, which involved
wrapping her entire body except her head
and one hand in red cloth and laying her
on a mattress in front of a fire. It worked.*

The last gasp

By 1602 Elizabeth was sixty-nine and a very weak old
woman. She became seriously ill with a quinsy, or
ulcer, in the throat. It was difficult and painful for her
to swallow and soon it developed into a soreness of
the lungs.

She sat on some cushions in
her chamber for four days,
hardly speaking. On the
third day she put one
of her fingers into
her mouth and
stayed staring
at the floor.

By the fourth day she was so weak and light that the doctors could carry her to her bed without any protests. Her councillors gathered round. They asked her if she would agree to James VI of Scotland, the son of Mary Queen of Scots, succeeding her on the throne. She appeared to agree. She had already written many kindly letters to him, advising him on how to run his kingdom.

Elizabeth I died about three o'clock in the morning of 24th March 1602 . She was buried in Westminster Abbey on April 28th. The streets were crowded with people and there was a general moaning and groaning.

So ended Elizabeth I, the last of the Tudors, the mother of modern England, and perhaps the greatest leader the country has ever had. It was hard to believe that she had gone; she had been Queen of England for forty-four years. Most people couldn't remember a time when she hadn't been queen.

At that time 24th March was the last day of the year.

SO WHAT HAPPENED NEXT?

HI!

WELL, A BIT OF IT

Robert Carey, Elizabeth's cousin, was nearby in Richmond Palace when she died. He walked quietly out of the palace grounds then mounted a horse and galloped up the Great North Road. Within sixty hours he had ridden nearly four hundred miles to Holyrood House in Edinburgh, on a relay of horses which were waiting along the road. He was the first person to bring news of Elizabeth's death to James VI of Scotland, heir to the English throne.

James set off for England within the week, with a large crowd of Scottish followers. The English greeted him happily – but they soon changed their minds. James I of England was the first of some seriously bad Stuart kings; by comparison, Elizabeth's reign was a truly golden age.

STATE THE DATE

GLORIANA AT A GLANCE

KIDS' STUFF

1533	Henry VIII marries Anne Boleyn
	Elizabeth is born
1536	Anne Boleyn is beheaded
	Henry marries Jane Seymour
1537	Edward VI is born
1547	Death of Henry VIII
	Elizabeth's sister, Mary, is crowned.
1549	Thomas Seymour beheaded
1554	Elizabeth sent to the Tower by Mary
1558	Mary dies
	Elizabeth crowned

QUEEN AT LAST

1559	Acts of Supremacy define Church of England
1561	Mary Queen of Scots sails to Scotland
1562	Elizabeth gets smallpox
1562-98	French Wars of Religion
1565	Mary Queen of Scots marries Darnley
1566	David Rizzio murdered
1567	Darnley murdered, Mary Queen of Scots marries Bothwell
	Mary escapes to England

1568	Dutch uprising against Spaniards begins
1572	Saint Bartholemew's Day Massacre
1577-1580	Drake's voyage round the World
1579	Francis, Duke of Alencon, visits England to woo Elizabeth
1587	Drake destroys Spanish fleet in Cadiz Harbour
	Mary Queen of Scots beheaded
1588	Armada defeated
	Dashing Dudley, Earl of Leicester, dies

THE LAST GASP

1597	Early flush toilet installed at Richmond Palace
1598	William Cecil dies
1599	Globe Theatre first built
	Essex goes to Ireland
1600	East India Company founded
1601	Essex beheaded
1602	Elizabeth died
	James VI of Scotland became James I of England

GRAND QUIZ

Now that you've finished my book why not test your Elizabethan expertise? Answers on page 124.

SECTION I – ELIZABETH, THE EARLY YEARS

1) How did Elizabeth's father, Henry VIII, feel about her birth?

a) He was delighted, he'd always wanted a girl.
b) He was very miffed, he'd hoped for a boy.
c) He wasn't bothered either way, just pleased to have a baby.

2) Which of these subjects were generally taught to upper-class Tudor girls?

a) short-hand
b) dancing and music, amongst other things
c) horticulture and farming

SECTION 2 – THE TUDOR ECONOMY

3) What was England's biggest
   export during Tudor Times?

a) Wool
b) Tabby cats
c) Industrial machinery

4) Who brought the potato to England?

   a) Sir Francis Drake
   b) Sir Walter Raleigh
   c) An angry Inuit

5) What sort of work did Tudor women do?

a) They never did any work outside the
   home.
b) Sometimes they did jobs like baker
   as well as housework.
c) They were at the top of the power pyramid
   and therefore never did any work at all.

6) Who was a nightsoil man?

   a) A gardener who worked late at nght
   b) Someone who emptied peoples' toilets
   c) A dirty soldier

SECTION 3 – LAW AND ORDER

7) Who were known for carrying off
   widows?

a) Welshmen
b) Protestant clegymen
c) The landless poor

8) Who were Upright Men?

a) The leaders of robber bands
b) Protestant clergymen
c) Members of Elizabeth's Privy Council

9) Who was Francis Throckmorton?

a) A Catholic conspirator who was
   horribly tortured after his capture
b) The Royal Valet in charge of
   Elizabeth's frocks
c) A Protestant clergyman

SECTION 4 – TUDOR LIFESTYLES

10) Which of these was a codpiece?

a) A helping of fried fish
b) A men's fashion accessory
c) A type of wig worn by Elizabeth

11) Which of these animals was a top Tudor pet?

a) A peacock
b) A hedgehog
c) A tabby cat

12) Which group of people were especially vunerable
   to green-sickness?

a) People who ate too many vegetables
b) Young girls who didn't get enough
   iron in their diet
c) Noblemen who got their fingers
   stained from counting their
   money too much

123

Section 5 – The End

13) *Find the odd one out...*which one of these people was *not* beheaded during Elizabeth's lifetime?

a) Queen Anne Boleyn
b) Lord Thomas Seymour
c) Mary, Queen of Scots
d) Robert Devereux, Earl of Essex
e) Sir Francis Drake

14) Who succeeded Elizabeth to the throne?

a) Edward VI
b) The Earl of Essex
c) James VI of Scotland

ANSWERS:

1. b) see page 6
2. b) see pages 12-14
3. a) see page 65
4. b) see page 37
5. b) see page 49
6. b) see page 30
7. a) see page 67
8. a) see page 69
9. a) see page 59
10. b) see page 47
11. c) see pages 32 and 18. (Tudors ate hedgehogs and peacocks!).
12. b) see page 114
13. e) Drake beheaded a mutinous gentleman in his crew but was not beheaded himself, see page 91. The others were all beheaded.
14. c) see page 118

124

INDEX

What They Don't Tell You About...
ORDER FORM

0 340 71330 5	ART	£3.99
0 340 63622 X	QUEEN VICTORIA	£3.99
0 340 69349 5	LIVING THINGS	£3.99
0 340 67093 2	SHAKESPEARE	£3.99
0 340 69350 9	STORY OF SCIENCE	£3.99
0 340 65614 X	ANCIENT EGYPTIANS	£3.99
0 340 68611 1	VIKINGS	£3.99
0 340 68612 X	WORLD WAR II	£3.99
0 340 70922 7	ROMANS	£3.99
0 340 70921 9	ANGLO SAXONS	£3.99
0 340 71329 1	PLANET EARTH	£3.99
0 340 71328 3	ANCIENT GREEKS	£3.99
0 340 68995 1	STORY OF MUSIC	£3.99
0 340 73611 9	OLYMPICS	£3.99
0 340 78805 4	WORLD WAR I	£3.99
0 340 78806 2	CHARLES I AND THE CIVIL WAR	£3.99
0 340 78807 0	THE COLD WAR	£3.99

All Hodder Children's books are available at your local bookshop or newsagent, or can be ordered direct from the publisher. Just write to the address below. Prices and availability subject to change without notice.

Hodder Children's Books, Cash Sales Department, Bookpoint, 130 Milton Park, Abingdon, Oxon, OX14 4SB, UK.
Email address: orders@bookpoint.co.uk

Please enclose a cheque or postal order made payable to Bookpoint Ltd to the value of the cover price and allow the following for postage and packing:
UK & BFPO - £1.00 for the first book, 50p for the second book, and 30p for each additional book ordered, up to a maximum charge of £3.00.
OVERSEAS & EIRE - £2.00 for the first book, £1.00 for the second book, and 50p for each additional book.

If you have a credit card you may order by telephone - (01235) 400414 (lines open 9 am - 6 pm, Monday to Saturday; 24 hour message answering service). Alternatively you can send a fax on 01235 400454.